Collaborative Peer Review:

The Role of Faculty in Improving College Teaching

by Larry Keig and Michael D. Waggoner

ASHE-ERIC Higher Education Report No. 2, 1994

Prepared by

Clearinghouse on Higher Education
The George Washington University

In cooperation with

ASHE

Association for the Study
of Higher Education

Published by

Graduate School of Education and Human Development
The George Washington University

Jonathan D. Fife, Series Editor

Cite as
Keig, Larry, and Michael D. Waggoner. 1994. *Collaborative Peer Review: The Role of Faculty in Improving College Teaching.* ASHE-ERIC Higher Education Report No. 2. Washington, D.C.: The George Washington University, School of Education and Human Development.

Library of Congress Catalog Card Number 94-73328
ISSN 0884-0040
ISBN 1-878380-58-3

Managing Editor: Bryan Hollister
Manuscript Editor: Alexandra Rockey
Cover design by Michael David Brown, Rockville, Maryland

The ERIC Clearinghouse on Higher Education invites individuals to submit proposals for writing monographs for the *ASHE-ERIC Higher Education Report* series. Proposals must include:
1. A detailed manuscript proposal of not more than five pages.
2. A chapter-by-chapter outline.
3. A 75-word summary to be used by several review committees for the initial screening and rating of each proposal.
4. A vita and a writing sample.

ERIC **Clearinghouse on Higher Education**
School of Education and Human Development
The George Washington University
One Dupont Circle, Suite 630
Washington, DC 20036-1183

This publication was prepared partially with funding from the Office of Educational Research and Improvement, U.S. Department of Education, under contract no. ED RR-93-0200. The opinions expressed in this report do not necessarily reflect the positions or policies of OERI or the Department.

EXECUTIVE SUMMARY

*Unless faculty members are willing to leave the evaluation
of teaching to students, who possess only a limited view,
or to administrators, who often don't have the time or necessary background, then they must be willing to invest their
time in efforts in peer evaluation of teaching* (Centra 1986,
p. 1).

Teaching is "the business of the business—the activity that
is central to all colleges and universities" (Pew Higher Education Research Program 1989, p. 1). But teaching is not
always taken seriously and too often is relegated to a position
below that of other professional activities. While there unques-
tionably is superior teaching in the academy, nearly everyone
agrees that it could be improved significantly and that the
teaching of even the best faculty could be strengthened.

What Arguments Can Be Made for Implementing Programs to Improve Teaching, Apart From the Personnel Decision-Making Process? For Faculty Colleague Involvement in Instructional Improvement?

For decades, academicians have assumed, usually erroneously,
that summative evaluation—decision making with respect
to reappointment, promotion, tenure, and compensation—
is also a means by which instructional improvement can be
facilitated. In practice, summative evaluation rarely provides
sufficient information to faculty for improving teaching. In
recent years, in fact, time-honored practices of faculty evaluation have been criticized as "shoddy, intellectually sloppy,
slipshod, and such a . . . source of shame that it is hardly surprising that teaching is rarely rewarded in an appropriate way"
(Scriven 1980, p. 7), as "simplistic," "primitive," and "without
significant credibility" (Soderberg 1986, p. 23), and as "generally quite limited, sporadic, and inadequate" (Dressel 1976,
p. 333).

   In response to this criticism, scholars have recommended
that formative evaluation—assessment specifically designed
to improve teaching—be put into place alongside, but apart
from, summative evaluation. Other scholars have suggested
that formative peer evaluation, a process in which faculty work
collaboratively to assess each others' teaching and to assist
one another in efforts to strengthen teaching, be developed
and implemented.

   Collaborative peer review probably should include opportunities for faculty to learn how to teach more effectively, to practice new teaching techniques and approaches, to get regular feedback on their classroom performance, and to receive coaching from colleagues (Menges 1985). The thrust, thus, is developmental—a process providing "data, diagnostic, and descriptive feedback, with which to improve instruction" (Weimer, Kerns, and Parrett 1988)—not judgmental.

Peer review should be a component of formative evaluation of teaching because informed faculty have knowledge of subject matter, teaching and learning, students, institutional culture, and their colleagues' teaching that is uniquely theirs, apart from information administrators, teaching consultants, and students can provide. It is becoming obvious to increasing numbers of faculty that successful teachers are not only experts in their fields of study but also knowledgeable about teaching strategies and learning theories and styles, committed to the personal and intellectual development of their students, cognizant of the complex contexts in which teaching and learning occur, and concerned about colleagues' as well as their own teaching. And it also is becoming increasingly obvious to faculty that they have strengths and weaknesses in these areas, and that many of them could be of assistance to and helped by colleagues.

What Aspects of Teaching Are Faculty More Qualified To Assess than Students and Other Constituencies of The Academic Community?

Faculty can evaluate their colleagues' performance at three stages of instruction: pre-interaction, delivery, and post-interaction. They can also assess interrelationships among the aforementioned stages and the following processes: goals and objectives, methods and materials, and feedback (Soderberg 1986). In addition, faculty can critique colleagues' teaching on the basis of criteria that are appropriate for this complex professional activity. According to Scriven, there are four such criteria: quality of content taught, the instructor's success in teaching that content and in inspiring student learning, the instructor's mastery of professional skills in writing tests and in evaluating the academic work of students, and the instructor's adherence to ethical standards (1985, p. 36).

Cohen and McKeachie's classification of the roles faculty should play in assessing colleagues' teaching is a particularly useful outline (1980). These roles are: elements of course design, including goals, content, and organization; methods and materials used in delivery of instruction; evaluation of students' academic work and the instructor's grading practices; and integration and interpretation of information gathered from students, administrators, and self-assessment as well as from peers.

What Methods Should Be Used by Faculty to Assess Colleagues' Teaching, When the Purpose of the Evaluation Is Instructional Improvement?

A number of methods have been employed in formative peer evaluation. They include direct classroom observation, video-taping of classes, evaluation of course materials, an assessment of instructor evaluation of the academic work of students, and analysis of teaching portfolios. Hart has identified six instructional events occurring during delivery that should be critiqued by knowledgeable colleagues:

1. The place where and the time when classes are taught and other physical factors affecting delivery;
2. The procedures used by the teacher in conducting the class;
3. The teacher's use of language to inform, explain, persuade, and motivate, and the language students use in respond-ing and reacting to the teacher;
4. The roles played by teacher and students as they interact;
5. The relationship of what is occurring in a particular class to other classes, disciplines, and the curriculum in general; and
6. The outcomes of teaching, as reflected in student learning (1987).

Other scholars (Elbow 1980; Katz and Henry 1988) recom-mend that classroom observation be combined with faculty interviews with individual students or groups of students.

Videotaping of classes should be employed for its unique potential in improving teaching: validating feedback from other sources (Perlberg 1983), documenting and preserving the strengths of teachers, identifying weaknesses, and com-paring teaching at different points in teachers' careers (Lichty and Peterson 1979). In formative peer evaluation, video play-back/feedback should be considered more than an alternative to classroom observation.

Informed peers are ideally suited to assess colleagues' course materials and evaluation of students' academic work.

As McCarthey and Peterson suggest, these materials "provide an overview of the curriculum taught, information about teaching strategies, and details about assignments given. Materials can indicate types of communication with students . . . the kind of management system used, and resources provided to students. . . . There is a plausible logical connection between quality materials and quality classroom performance for many, but not all teachers" (1988, p. 261). Cohen and McKeachie's classification cited earlier is especially instructive in describing what materials faculty could examine and how to complete what otherwise might be a daunting task (1980).

Several program examples in which formative peer evaluation has been employed are described in some detail in the text. Readers are urged to consider each program carefully, for each has its worthy elements.

What Factors Can Detract from Faculty Members' Willingness to Participate in Programs Designed To Improve Teaching?

On the basis of the arguments presented thus far, it would appear that formative peer evaluation should be embraced for the betterment of the academy. We know, however, that use of this form of instructional improvement activity has been negligible. A number of reasons have been cited for the unwillingness of faculty to participate in the various methods of formative colleague assessment.

The disincentives include faculty attitudes toward academic freedom; their perceptions of the representativeness, accuracy, and typicality of what is evaluated; their conception of the objectivity of those who conduct the assessment; and their values with respect to the institution's rewards and incentives. Ways must be found to convince faculty that what they may consider disincentives can be opportunities for professional development. For example, having classes observed and materials assessed by colleagues for the purpose of instructional improvement should no more be considered a threat to academic freedom than would having colleagues critique a proposed manuscript for publication. And including videotaping of classes and peer review of course materials and of instructor evaluations of students' academic work, in addition to classroom observation, should make the process more credible to the faculty.

What Steps Can Be Taken to Enhance Programs To Improve Teaching So Faculty Will Avail Themselves of the Programming?

Scholars insist there are several ways of enhancing the process that will improve the likelihood faculty will develop and take part in formative peer evaluation. Besides convincing faculty that the "disincentives" can be opportunities rather than liabilities, the process might be enhanced by involving the faculty in the design and implementation of the program, in the establishment of standards of effective teaching upon which performance will be assessed, in programs that provide training in methods of supervision and communication, and in the interpretation and integration of data provided by students, administrators, and colleagues, as well as faculty members' self-assessment.

How Can Faculty, Students, and Colleges and Universities Benefit from Formative Peer Evaluation Of Teaching?

Scholars have suggested that a number of personal and institutional benefits might be realized from faculty participation in the formative peer evaluation of teaching. Researchers have found not only *that* but *how* teaching improves when faculty avail themselves of programs in which they work collaboratively to improve teaching. After taking part in such programs,

> *[Faculty] often develop a deeper interest in and commitment to being a good teacher and, through their exposure to theories of teaching and learning, consciously formulate personal philosophies about teaching. For many [faculty], the core of their emerging teaching philosophies is a humanism that emphasizes appreciation of student differences, interest in listening to students, and a greater commitment to fostering the process of students' intellectual growth than to dispensing knowledge. . . . This heightened sensitivity to students' diverse needs and challenges, coupled with the exploration of teaching and learning theory, often causes [faculty] to cultivate new approaches to their teaching* (Austin 1992a, p. 80).

Studies also appear to show that faculty morale and collegiality improve when faculty are involved in formative peer evaluation. While student learning may improve when faculty take part in such programs, that is a difficult claim to substantiate, since many variables besides teaching affect student learning. At this time, there is not enough evidence to suggest that the tenure status of junior faculty is enhanced when they have participated in formative peer evaluation.

What Recommendations Emerge From a Study of Formative Peer Evaluation?

The recommendations made at this point are, for the most part, general and broad-based; other, more specific recommendations are presented throughout the text.

1. Faculty evaluation should include largely separate formative and summative tracks. Summative evaluation, including rigorous quantitative and qualitative data gathering and analysis, is essential for maintaining the academy's integrity; formative evaluation, including equally rigorous descriptive strategies, along with ample feedback and opportunities for practice and coaching, is necessary for improving teaching.

2. Formative evaluation should include nonjudgmental descriptions of faculty members' teaching by colleagues, administrators, and, where available, teaching consultants as well as students; each constituency should be asked for data only in areas where it is qualified to provide it.

3. Faculty should be encouraged to take part in yearlong programs of formative peer evaluation of teaching every four or five years over the course of their academic careers; that encouragement should come from administrators and the senior faculty.

4. Faculty should take leadership in the design and implementation of programs of formative evaluation of teaching.

5. Faculty should be provided opportunities for training in the skills needed to conduct formative peer evaluation.

6. The involvement of the faculty in the formative evaluation of teaching should be guided by expertise in appropriate areas of the knowledge base of teaching; at the same time, care must be taken to minimize potential problems that can arise from having the same faculty involved in the formative and summative evaluation of a colleague.

7. Formative peer evaluation should include direct classroom observation, videotaping of classes, evaluation of course materials, an assessment of instructor evaluations of the academic work of students, and analysis of teaching port-

folios. In this process, it is advisable to use the methods in combination, not as independent entities.

8. Institutional rewards and incentives should be structured to demonstrate to faculty that participation in formative peer evaluation of teaching is truly valued.

9. Research should proceed along several potentially lucrative lines: the interaction of variables in specific institutional contexts; the tie between participation in formative peer evaluation and motivational theory; documentation and reporting experiences with formative peer assessment, whether they are succeeding or have failed; and rigorous empirical and ethnographic study of programs of formative peer evaluation currently in place.

CONTENTS

FOREWORD

It is a contradiction that, in an organization in which the primary activity is instruction, developing the skill of teaching and the recognition of good teachers is so undervalued. This contradiction has not been lost on the general public but, because of the lack of hard evidence to the contrary, the conventional opinion is that this contradiction seems to have made only the slightest dent in the consciousness of many academic leaders. In reality, this is not the case. Most, if not all, of higher education's academic leadership are abundantly aware of the importance of good teaching and the lack of education that graduate schools give their students concerning the research and practice of teaching. This awareness is not translated into specific results—not because faculty do not want to be good teachers, but because of the way academic leadership has allowed the arguments to be framed by the professorate and the lack of genuine rewards that the leadership provides for good teaching.

The primary barrier as seen by academic leaders is the restrictions caused by the concept of academic freedom reinforced by tenure. On the surface it appears that the shield of academic freedom is used by a faculty who want absolute freedom and minimal accountability. While faculty want to be protected from arbitrary action that will inhibit the free flow of ideas, surveys clearly show that they want to be good teachers. The shield of academic freedom is used because there is a genuine fear concerning the use and accuracy of the evaluations.

There are two separate and distinct bases for this fear. The first is faculty's experience with evaluations. Almost always, faculty have seen evaluations conducted to justify something negative. Therefore, most evaluations are used for criticism or to justify top-down administrative action. A second concern relates to the accuracy of evaluations of teaching. Most faculty realize they do not have adequate formal training to be outstanding teachers. What they have learned they have gained through modeling faculty they had as students and through their informal, on-the-job, hit-or-miss teaching experiences. Since they know they do not have the expertise to judge good teaching themselves, there is real doubt that administrators, who are even more untrained, would have better skills to evaluate teaching.

These two concerns are reinforced by the lack of action by academic leadership to specifically improve the atmosphere and conditions surrounding the evaluation of teaching. The concerns could be addressed in several ways.

- Require all doctoral students to receive training in the research and skill of teaching in their cognitive area.
- Make it part of the organizational culture that all faculty continuously will take courses and receive training to improve their knowledge and skill of teaching.
- Provide incentives, such as salary increments or bonuses, to encourage faculty to seek certification of increased teaching skills.
- Make all evaluation purely a formative or developmental process, thus eliminating the fear of improper use of teaching evaluation.

Asserting this type of major change in the way an institution addresses the importance of demonstrated teaching skill in its faculty cannot happen overnight. However, it is distinctly probable that private and public supports of higher education will begin to demand such changes. Many institutions have taken steps to prepare by making small, nonthreatening changes that will begin to positively affect the teaching culture of their institutions.

This report, written by Larry Keig, adjunct professor, and Michael D. Waggoner, associate professor and head of the department of educational administration and counseling at the University of Northern Iowa College of Education, examines ways in which institutions are affecting their teaching climate. Through the use of peer review of teaching, faculty involuntarily are seeking to improve their instructional skills. The authors begin by establishing rationales for formative evaluation, for peer review in instructional improvement efforts, and for a program of comprehensive faculty evaluation in which formative peer assessment is an essential component. They then examine the roles that might be played by peers in assessing colleague teaching and five methods peers have used to assist colleagues in efforts to improve instruction. After examining several programs involving different methods of peer review and factors that either detract from or encourage faculty willingness to participate in this form of evaluations, the authors conclude with a number of recommendations for the practice of formative peer evaluation of teaching.

The pressure on higher education to measurably demonstrate activity is increasing. Higher education is becoming more important to society and, therefore, society is less willing to allow "business as usual" to continue. Institutions may anticipate these demands and establish their own ways to develop evidence that they are being responsive to these expectations, or they can wait for external areas to force their measurement requirements. Demonstrating that faculty teaching skills continuously are being improved is one of the ways institutions can demonstrate their responsiveness to ensure the distinction of their institution. This report provides an excellent foundation for those institutions that see peer evaluation of faculty as one process that can help to make the culture more responsive to the evaluation and improvement of teaching.

Jonathan D. Fife
Series Editor, Professor of Higher Education Administration and Director, ERIC Clearinghouse on Higher Education

ACKNOWLEDGMENTS

This book evolved from the literature review of Dr. Larry Keig's doctoral dissertation. It would not have found its way into print had it not been for Dr. Mike Waggoner's early recognition, as a member of the dissertation committee, that an expanded treatment of the topic might be valuable to a wider academic community. Dr. Keig is grateful for Dr. Waggoner's encouragement, for it spearheaded a collaboration in which we have been able to examine the peer review of teaching, a joint working relationship extending well beyond the scope of the original study.

We believe that what may be valuable here has been strengthened by our collaboration and expect this line of work to continue for months and years to come. We encourage readers' comments and experiences with collaborative peer review of teaching.

The advice and assistance of other dissertation committee members are gratefully acknowledged: Dr. Dale Jackson, chair, for insights into the nature and process of college faculty evaluation and for his encouragement and enthusiasm during the writing process; Dr. Thomas Hansmeier, not only for the wise counsel of a seasoned administrator and mentor, but also for deft editing; Dr. Bruce Rogers, for help and patience in the conceptualization of the study; Dr. Basil Reppas, for a philosophical perspective and critical analysis; and Dr. Wylie Anderson, for an economist's "nonprofessional educator" viewpoint.

Dr. Keig is indebted to many former students, teachers, and colleagues for inspiring a lifelong interest   fascination, really   with teaching and learning and how these processes might be improved. They are not mentioned here by name, but surely they know who they are. Dr. Keig also has appreciated the support of several friends as the book took shape, particularly Philip and Wanda Batchelder, Francoise Dupuis, Dennis and Sharon Heth, Norman and Jane Seeman, Patsy Steffey, and David Vernon.

Both authors are grateful to Dr. David Walker, associate dean of the University of Northern Iowa Graduate College, for research grants to support this work. We express our sincere thanks to Cindy Haarstad, a master's degree student in the UNI Postsecondary Education: Student Affairs graduate program, for her significant role in preparing the manuscript with great care.

INTRODUCTION

Teaching is a complex web of acts, a fact to which those of us who stand in front of students in classrooms or who interact with students in other ways can readily attest. To be valuable to faculty, the evaluation of teaching must be sophisticated, systematic, and thorough, as well as flexible enough to capture the substance, essence, and nuances of the teaching process. For years, the primary emphasis in faculty evaluation has been on decision making relative to reappointment, promotion, tenure, and compensation. In most instances, professors' effectiveness as classroom teachers is but one element considered in making these judgments. Generally, it is doubtful that the personnel decision-making process has had much positive impact on improving teaching (Cross 1986; Dressel 1976; Hodgkinson 1972; Scriven 1980; Weimer, Parrett, and Kerns 1988).

Generally, it is doubtful that the personnel decision-making process has had much positive impact on improving teaching.

In assessing teaching, decision makers usually rely heavily—often too extensively—on student ratings of courses and instructors. We believe that when faculty and administrators allow student ratings to be the only real source of information about teaching, they unwittingly contribute to a system in which too much emphasis is placed on evaluating superficial teaching skills and not enough is placed on more substantive matters. Moreover, we believe faculty and administrators abnegate their professional responsibilities when they are unwilling to assess aspects of teaching they are particularly well-qualified to evaluate.

We argue here for a process for evaluating teaching that has as its end improvement of instruction—one in which faculty peers (and other qualified constituencies) provide information their colleagues might use to become better teachers. We are convinced that if faculty desire credible evaluation, they must create largely independent systems that promote teaching improvement and contribute to rational personnel decisions.

In this report, we look at how evaluation might be used for instructional improvement and, more specifically, at how peer review might be used for this purpose. First, we attempt to establish rationales for formative evaluation, for peer review in instructional improvement efforts, and for a program of comprehensive faculty evaluation in which formative peer evaluation is an essential component. Second, we examine the roles that might be played by peers in assessing their colleagues' teaching. Third, we look at five methods in which peers have been involved in efforts to improve the teaching of their colleagues. Fourth, we describe programs involving peer review. Fifth, we consider factors that may detract from faculty members' willingness to participate in this form of evaluation. Sixth, we examine factors that may improve the likelihood of faculty involvement and enhance the process. Seventh, we consider how their participation may affect teaching, learning, and faculty morale and collegiality. Finally, we present a number of recommendations for the practice of formative peer evaluation in higher education.

State of College Teaching

Teaching is, it has been said, "the business of the business" of higher education. We also are told that:

> *Too seldom is collegiate teaching viewed for what it is: . . . the activity that is central to all colleges and universities. . . . Teaching is the task that distinguishes colleges and universities, along with primary and secondary schools, from all other service agencies* (Pew 1989, pp. 1-2).

In many colleges and universities, teaching and related activities are subordinated to other academic responsibilities, especially research and publication (Boyer 1987; Carnegie Foundation 1990a, 1990b; Fairweather 1993; Ladd 1979; Miller 1990; Pew 1989, 1990; Scriven 1980; Soderberg 1985; Study Group 1984). Calls are being made by government officials, by the general public, in the popular press, and from within the academy itself to establish once again the role of teaching as the primary responsibility of colleges and universities.

By nearly all accounts, teaching in colleges and universities is not as good as it should be. There are, no doubt, many reasons to explain why faculty do not always teach as well as they could. We discuss six factors that have been cited as reasons for less-than-effective teaching.

First, it is difficult to refute claims that teaching has been neglected by many professors, due in part to a reward structure that puts an undue premium on traditional scholarly activities and devalues teaching. Yet, even at liberal arts colleges where teaching is the preeminent faculty role, there still is plenty of poor teaching. Clearly, then, not all of the blame for ineffective teaching can be laid on the academy's reward structure. We return to this issue in the sections on disincentives and incentives.

A second factor is the erroneous assumption "that teaching a subject matter requires only that one know it" (Eble 1988, p. 24). A number of voices have responded to this of late, among them this one, noting that:

> *Advanced knowledge of a subject is not itself a sufficient preparation to teach students. . . . Advanced degree holders or candidates are largely content with believing that one simply teaches by doing, an attitude of being somehow above conscious pedagogy* (Pew 1990, p. 5).

Said another way:

> *A body of knowledge is essential. But it is of limited value without . . . an understanding of how learning occurs. . . . The success of the classroom enterprise depends both on the teacher's communication of knowledge and his or her ability to help students construct their own knowledge. It depends on the teacher's skill in encouraging dialogue and in probing students' understanding: provoking, questioning, guiding, and interpreting* (Pew 1989, pp. 3-4).

A third, more basic factor that may explain why teaching is not as good as it could be is the mistaken notion that teachers are born and not made. Shulman insists that a successful teacher learns how to teach, and continues to learn, by studying not only in a specific content area but also in fields related to teaching (history, philosophy, psychology, and sociology, for example) and in the liberal arts (1987, 1989). The general areas in which teachers need to be well-versed in order to promote student learning are:

- Content knowledge;
- General pedagogical knowledge, with special references to those broad principles and strategies of classroom management and organization that appear to transcend subject matter;
- Curriculum knowledge, with particular grasp of the materials and programs that serve as "tools of the trade" for teachers;
- Pedagogical content knowledge, that special amalgam of content and pedagogy that is uniquely the province

of teachers, their own professional form of professional understandings;

- Knowledge of learners and their characteristics;
- Knowledge of educational contexts, ranging from the workings of the group or classroom, the governance and finance of [education], to the character of communities and cultures; and
- Knowledge of educational ends, purposes, and values, and their philosophical and historical grounds (Shulman 1987).

Acquiring breadth and depth of knowledge in these areas will, Shulman says, enhance the likelihood that faculty will develop the competencies that will allow them to communicate, with increasing sophistication, what they know to their students. The competencies, which are influenced by all the teacher has experienced as well as virtually everything he or she has studied, encompass the teacher's abilities to:

- Comprehend both content and purposes (p. 15);
- Transform the content knowledge he or she possesses into forms that are pedagogically powerful and yet adaptive to the varieties in ability and in background presented by the students (p. 15);
- [Organize and manage] the classroom, [present] clear explanations and vivid descriptions, [assign and check] work, and [interact] effectively with students through questions and probes, answers and reactions, and praise and criticism (p. 17);
- Check for understanding and misunderstanding . . . while teaching interactively, as well as [by] more formal testing and evaluation that teachers do to provide feedback and give grades (pp. 18-19);
- [Reflect on] the teaching and learning that has occurred, and [reconstruct, reenact, and/or recapture] the events, the emotions, and the accomplishments (p. 19); and
- Arrive at a new beginning . . . with new comprehension, both of the purposes and of the subjects to be taught, and also of the students and of the processes of pedagogy themselves (p. 19).

Also recognizing that subject-matter mastery is but one competency required of effective teachers, Yarbrough lists a range of capabilities, skills, and behaviors that are essential for developing expertise in teaching (1988). These competencies, or "dimensions of knowledge," are:

1. Subject-matter content knowledge
2. Subject-matter pedagogical knowledge
3. Curricular knowledge
4. General pedagogical knowledge
5. Knowledge of learner characteristics
6. Knowledge of communication techniques

Yarbrough goes even further, noting that:

> It is not enough to say that expert teachers possess expert knowledge in the content of their subject matter, in pedagogical principles, in principles of learning, and in specific knowledge of their students' current knowledge, capabilities, and limitations. It also requires that expert teachers have the capability to process information from multiple dimensions in concert and to apply that information to new and potentially unique problems in the teaching process (p. 223).

Yarbrough's "dimensions of knowledge" are not too different from Shulman's "pedagogy of substance" (1987). Yarbrough, in addition, explores an experiential dimension as well, observing that:

> Expert teachers (based on peer nominations) are more likely to perceive a very brief sequence of events in a classroom as supplying a wealth of information to be interpreted in reference to various domains of stored knowledge. Beginning teachers viewing the same sequence of events interpreted the events in a unidimensional fashion. It appears that expert teachers have automatic procedures that reference teaching events, even at the procedural level, to more diverse domains of knowledge than do beginning teachers (p. 224).

Clearly, there is more to effective teaching than having a command of subject matter, as essential as that is. Ways must be found, through graduate school training and inservice programming, to help teachers develop other requisite competencies.

A fourth factor likely to limit instructional effectiveness is a teacher's unwillingness to take differences among students into account. As Katz and Henry observe:

Though students are not all alike, teaching continues on the assumption of a common denominator that, when found, will enable the faculty member to reach most of the students. Those faculty who have given up aiming for the middle range of their students have resorted either to addressing primarily those few students who seem likely to catch on to their particular perspective and level of thinking or to focusing on those students who need the most help to make it through the particular course. Some faculty have given up altogether on determining a strategy for coping with student differences and simply run their course on a sink-or-swim basis, counting on the "objectivity" of their grading system to maintain "standards" and thus avoiding the fact of student diversity. As the numbers of students in college classrooms have risen over the years, the probability and the possibility of attending to student differences have decreased. When classes are small, and some give-and-take discussion is encouraged between the teacher and the students, it is more difficult to overlook differences among students. But with large classes and the use of the lecture method, the fact of individual differences is much less evident and these differences can be rather easily ignored (1988, p. 111).

A fifth factor that may limit more effective teaching is, according to Shulman, the locus from which teaching improvement efforts often emanate (1993). He contends that programs initiated by universitywide "centers," while praiseworthy in many ways, may militate against making teaching "community property" in which decisions about "quality, control, judgment, evaluation, and paradigmatic definitions" rightfully are made by members of each community (namely, faculty in the various academic fields on campus) (p. 6). Shulman contends that:

We need to reconnect teaching to the disciplines. Although the disciplines are easy to bash because of the many problems they create for us, they are, nevertheless, the basis for our intellectual communities. Like it or not, the forms of scholarship that are seen as intellectual work in the disciplines are going to be valued more than the forms of scholarship (like teaching) that are seen as non-disciplinary. . . .

Institutional support for teaching and its improvement tends to lie in a university center for teaching and learning . . . where faculty—regardless of department—can go for assistance in improving their practice. That's a perfectly reasonable idea. But notice the message it conveys—that teaching is generic, technical, and a matter of performance; that it's not part of the community that means so much to most faculty, the disciplinary, interdisciplinary, professional community. It's something general you lay on top of what you really do as a scholar in a discipline. . . . We need to make the review, examination, and support of teaching the responsibility of the disciplinary community (1993, p. 6).

Finally, as Miller reminds us, "That [while] good teaching is often a matter of instinct as it be personality, it is also a matter of hard work: discipline, perseverance, and the insight and inspiration that derive from intense moments or hours of celebration" (1990, p. 59). Or, as Menges more bluntly puts it, "Some faculty resist working hard on their teaching" (1980, p. 27).

There are many ways in which teaching could be improved. Too few teachers have examined in a systematic way how they teach or have thought about it seriously or reflectively. And they rarely get the help they need to improve from those who are in the best position to provide it: informed peers, teaching consultants, and administrators. In this report, we hope to establish our premise that our colleagues have unique abilities, apart from consultants, administrators, and students, that can help us improve our teaching.

State of the Evaluation of College Teaching

Arguments for and against the usefulness of evaluations of college teachers and teaching, the value of different methods of evaluation, and the suitability of various constituencies in assessing the instructional effectiveness of faculty have been occurring for decades. Regardless of the debate, faculty have been and continue to be evaluated, formally or informally, by individuals or groups of people. These judgments affect faculty members' personal and professional relationships with students, administrators, and colleagues and often also their reappointment, promotion, tenure, and compensation.

Cohen and McKeachie (1980) and Scriven (1980) argue that it is in the best interest of the faculty to have a formal, systematic program of faculty evaluation in place, because it can protect faculty from unjust personnel decisions. Lee (1982), Smith (1981), and Stevens (1985) suggest that such a program is also in the best interest of colleges and universities, since it can demonstrate that the process has been handled rationally, rather than arbitrarily or capriciously, when personnel decisions unfavorable to faculty are litigated. These recommendations refer specifically to summative evaluation—decision making relative to reappointment, promotion, tenure, and compensation—which emphasizes judgments about, not improvement of, performance.

Whether carried out formally or informally, effectively or ineffectively, summative evaluation has been, and remains, the principal method by which to evaluate teachers. For a long time, it has been assumed that this type of evaluation also would function instrumentally to improve teaching. But the notion that there is a direct relationship between summative evaluation and instructional improvement has been challenged in recent years. As indicated earlier, there is widespread agreement that this time-honored practice of evaluation has not significantly improved teaching. In decrying prevailing practices of faculty evaluation, Scriven has written that these approaches often are so "shoddy, intellectually sloppy, slipshod, and such a . . . source of shame, that it is hardly surprising that teaching is rarely rewarded in an appropriate way" (1980, p. 7). Less acerbic, but equally critical, Soderberg describes usual approaches as "simplistic" (1986, p. 13), "primitive," and "without significant credibility" (p. 23). Similarly, Dressel refers to common practices as "generally quite limited, sporadic, and inadequate" (1976, p. 333).

Assessment emphasizing instructional improvement has been derived recently in higher education. While interest in this form of evaluation is perhaps at an all-time high, the interest has waxed and waned over the years. All the while, however, influential scholars in the fields of teaching and student learning have continued to promote the idea that formative evaluation—assessment specifically designed to improve teaching—should become a regular part of the process of evaluation (Cross 1986; Dressel 1976; Hodgkinson 1972; Katz and Henry 1988; Sorcinelli 1984; Weimer 1990).

Motivating faculty to improve their classroom teaching may be positively affected to a degree by rewards dispensed or withheld through summative evaluation. But it also is said that extrinsic rewards (such as promotion, tenure, and salary increases) simply reinforce, rather than improve, performance (Hodgkinson 1972) or even reduce faculty motivation to teach effectively (McKeachie 1982). And the common faculty complaint that summative evaluation does not adequately assess their performance also may diminish its value in improving their teaching.

Proponents of formative evaluation are convinced that it is more promising than summative evaluation for motivating faculty to improve their teaching. Scholars also suggest that programs of instructional improvement should be a much more important institutional priority. Rationale for formative evaluation, for peer involvement in formative evaluation, and for a comprehensive program of faculty evaluation are presented next.

The importance of making fair and impartial personnel decisions cannot be disputed. Yet, decisions of this type are made only periodically, usually relatively early in a faculty member's career. Surely an equally if not more compelling reason for evaluating courses and instructors is to improve performance in progress. If a goal of evaluation is instructional improvement, it probably will be necessary, as Licata suggests, to evaluate teaching, research, and service not just when personnel decisions have to be made but more regularly throughout faculty members' careers, early in their appointments and at various midpoints and later in their tenure (1986). By doing so, colleges and universities might demonstrate more convincingly to students, parents/guardians, faculty, and other constituencies that teaching, teaching improvement, faculty growth, and faculty development are important institutional priorities.

Until recently, information about the effectiveness of teachers has come almost exclusively from student evaluations of courses and instructors. At many—perhaps most—colleges and universities, reliance on student ratings for this information is still the rule rather than the exception. The idea that other constituencies, especially a faculty member's peers and academic administrators, may have relevant information about faculty members' teaching has only begun to be explored. Data provided by each of these constituencies may be unique, all of it necessary if significant instructional improvement is to occur.

Inasmuch as there are different purposes for evaluating faculty (formative, summative, and perhaps others) as well as several constituencies who can assess specific aspects of faculty performance, there seems to be a need for more comprehensive faculty evaluation. In this section, we look more closely at rationales for formative evaluation, for peer review as one element in that process, and for comprehensive faculty evaluation. We also look at three models that involve formative peer evaluation.

The idea that a faculty member's peers and academic administrators may have relevant infomation about faculty members' teaching has only begun to be explored.

Rationale for the Formative Evaluation of Teaching

In higher education, faculty evaluation is carried out primarily for decisions regarding reappointment, promotion, tenure, and compensation and only secondarily, if at all, for improving performance. By necessity, all faculty roles—research and service as well as teaching—are accounted for when personnel decisions are made. During these deliberations, faculty usually are evaluated according to common standards.

In formative evaluation, the emphasis is on development, where efforts toward improvement can be directed toward any or all professional roles. If so desired, emphasis can be placed on instructional improvement, and faculty differences in educational philosophy and teaching style can be taken into account.

In commenting on instructional development within a broader context of faculty development, Menges points out some of the benefits of assessment expressly designed for teaching improvement:

> *Development [is] a natural process, an unfolding, gradual and continual. [It is] highly individual; it proceeds differently from person to person and from setting to setting. Its initiation is usually from within, although certain external circumstances support it more effectively than others. . . .*

> *We have had some success in identifying conditions under which faculty members are likely to learn about and adopt new instructional approaches. . . . These conditions include exposure to relevant theory, provision for practicing the new approaches and receiving feedback on the practice, and opportunities to be coached while applying the new approaches in the field. (Note the happy coincidence that these conditions for faculty are similar to conditions which promote learning and transfer for students in our classes.)* (1985, pp. 181-82)

Provisions for learning about teaching, practice in implementing new approaches and techniques, feedback to faculty on their efforts, and coaching from colleagues or consultants normally are not part of the process of faculty evaluation, although increasing numbers of scholars and practitioners believe there should be means available for doing so. While there may be resistance from faculty to involve themselves in another professional activity (Menges 1985), there probably are ways to motivate faculty to take advantage of formative evaluation of this type, although the type of motivation very well may differ among faculty members (Bess 1982).

Many scholars criticize the lack of relationship between faculty evaluation and teaching improvement. That sentiment is expressed succinctly by Aubrecht, who says, "Very few institutions are making good use of their faculty evaluation systems for development purposes" (1984, p. 88).

A number of scholars now recognize the need for formative as well as summative evaluation. Most of them recommend that the two functions be kept distinctly separate. Others believe that information gathered in summative evaluation also can be used for formative evaluation. Scholars almost unanimously agree that it is unwise and counterproductive to use information collected in formative evaluation in making personnel decisions.

The view that summative and formative evaluation should be separate entities in the assessment process is a common one. This notion is expressed in two pieces of recent scholarship. In a particularly strong voice, Cross describes fundamental differences between formative and summative evaluation:

> *Ironically, practically all the proposals and practices in assessment today involve summative evaluation. . . . There are few proposals for formative evaluation to show us how to improve education in process. . . . If we are to improve the quality of education, perhaps the most important question . . . to address is what decisions should be made to improve instruction. . . . How students are taught lies at the heart of quality education. It makes the difference between a lifelong learner and a grade grubber, between enthusiasm for learning and indifference to it, between an educated society and a credentialed one* (1986, pp. 3-4).

Weimer, Kerns, and Parrett are more direct in explaining why summative and formative evaluation require different types of information, suggesting why instructional improvement is unlikely to occur from summative evaluation:

> *It is the intent of summative evaluation to provide the comparative data for subsequent use in personnel decisions. These evaluations typically consist of items that describe teaching in global terms. . . . Whereas the intent of formative evaluation is to provide data, diagnostic and descriptive feedback, with which to improve instruction. . . .*
>
> *The purposes of the evaluations are different. Consequently the items on formative evaluation instruments and the items*

*on summative evaluations should differ also. . . . When
items do not correspond with the intended purposes of the
evaluation, e.g., providing summative data with the expec-
tation that the data will be used to improve, the potential
value of the evaluation process is attenuated* (1988, p. 286).

That admonition notwithstanding, there are those who argue
that data gathered for summative evaluation can be used for
instructional improvement. Dressel, for example, suggests
that "assessment activity must be broadly conceived as a basis
for improvement, not for making personnel decisions. Evaluation can be linked to reward structures, but with recognition
that improvement and development are the first concerns"
(1976, p. 374).

Writing alone a year before collaborating with others (Weimer, Kerns, and Parrett 1988), Weimer seems to strike a position somewhere between complete separation of summative
and formative evaluation and a linking of those functions. In
that provocative piece, she recommends:

> *Separate formative and summative evaluation activities,
> but link the results. The two activities should run on separate
> tracks with points of convergence at the beginning and end.
> Summative evaluation constructs the comprehensive picture
> of instructional competency. Formative evaluation closes
> in on the picture, dissects the component parts, analyzes
> the relationship to one another, identifies what parts should
> be changed, and provides initial feedback on the success
> of those changes. Summative evaluation occurs again to
> create another composite picture, this time to show the dif-
> ferences. The connection between the two cannot be over-
> emphasized. Formative evaluation must target appropriate
> areas of change. Summative assessment must reflect the
> impact of those changes* (1987, p. 10).

Rationale for Peer Review in the Formative Evaluation of Teaching

Several scholars believe that college teaching could be improved significantly if faculty worked collaboratively to that
end. While acknowledging there are still those who think
command of subject matter is all that is required to teach,
scholars say that faculty are becoming increasingly aware that

successful teachers are knowledgeable about teaching strategies and learning theories, committed to the individual development of students, cognizant of the complex contexts in which instruction occurs, and concerned about colleagues' teaching as well as their own. Every teacher has strengths and weaknesses in these areas, and many of them could assist and/or be helped by colleagues. All of this suggests that good teaching is developed over time and rarely is fully actualized. In short, college teaching will improve when faculty support each other with expertise that is uniquely theirs, apart from what students, teaching consultants, and academic administrators can contribute to instructional improvement (Batista 1976; Centra 1975, 1986, 1993; Cohen and McKeachie 1980; Hart 1987; Mathis 1974; Seldin 1984).

A number of the academy's conventions—epistemological, cultural, political, and practical factors that may undermine efforts to improve teaching—underscore a need for formative evaluation and for peer involvement in that process. These conventions include: the lack of agreement on what good teaching is; the inflexibility built into most systems of evaluation; the isolation of professors from one another with regard to teaching; the reluctance of faculty to seek help from colleagues with more expertise and experience and with higher status; and a reward structure in which research is more valued than teaching.

Abrami (1985), McKeachie (1986), Smith and Walvoord (1993), and others have observed that scholars do not agree, and probably never will, on what good teaching is and on how to evaluate it. It is not surprising, then, that faculty develop idiosyncratic teaching styles based on personal preferences and normative assumptions rather than on a uniform, codified standard of exemplary practice (Bulcock 1984; McKeachie 1986). For that reason, informed peers—who know their colleagues personally and professionally, are familiar with effective and ineffective practice in specific fields of study, and recognize that effective teaching is contingent upon a number of complex factors, only some of which can be controlled by instructors—may be especially forceful catalysts in the process of instructional improvement (Mathis 1974; Soderberg 1986).

Because teaching is so complex, scholars often criticize the rigidity of systems of evaluation based upon superficial style characteristics. In envisioning a more flexible alternative,

Cancelli proposes a system of assessment that:

makes minimal assumptions regarding how instruction should occur. It is left to the professional judgments of the professors to determine how they wish to develop and teach their courses. The system only requires that they be within the bounds of acceptable practice, broadly defined, that they do what they say they do, and that there be a cogent rationale for their choices. Thus, the review of each professor is unique and requires decisions based on disparate and often idiosyncratic bits of information. The use of judgments by peers provides a method that is flexible enough to adjust to the unique data base generated in each review (1987, p. 12).

It is relatively uncommon for teachers at any level—whether in elementary and secondary schools or in colleges and universities—to work collaboratively in improving teaching (Copeland and Jamgochian 1985; Johnson, Johnson, and Smith 1991; Katz and Henry 1988; Shulman 1993), though collaborative relationships probably are more common in the K-12 sector than in higher education. Copeland and Jamgochian note:

The isolation of teachers to meet together outside the classroom is a well-documented phenomena. . . . It is rare for two teachers to meet together outside of class time to discuss substantive issues related to their students or their own teaching. Systematic analysis of teaching, exploration of alternative approaches, analysis of individual teaching and learning problems, and the generation of and testing of possible solutions are all activities that typically occur at the individual teacher level, not among colleagues (p. 18).

Copeland and Jamgochian suggest that a number of institutional factors, including scheduling, task description, and administrative expectations, militate against a more collegial working relationship with respect to the teaching role. The isolation prompted by these institutional constraints often is exacerbated by teachers themselves who, for whatever reasons, feel uncomfortable opening up their classrooms to or frankly discussing issues about teaching with colleagues. The reasons for this resistance are varied. Some faculty insist that classrooms are their private domain. Others find, as Menges suggests, disparities in expertise, experience, or status between themselves and colleagues intimidating or threatening (1987). Others, though, may be uncomfortable working in formal relationships with professional staff developers, preferring instead "a close and informal relationship with a peer" (Menges 1987, p. 83; see also Braskamp 1978, pp. 2-3).

Differences in status can be overcome, however, if there is candor in acknowledging problems and in acting on the need to improve. In one successful instance,

> *a senior professor and department chair discovered, much to his chagrin, that student evaluations indicated room for substantial improvement in his teaching. At the next department meeting he put his concerns frankly before his colleagues and asked for their assistance in identifying what and how he could improve. He shared teaching materials, discussed his current teaching methods, and invited his colleagues to observe him in the classroom. Once his colleagues understood the seriousness of his request, they did as he asked, visiting his classroom, talking to his students, reviewing both the structure and the organization of his courses. The entire group shared and discussed together the teaching evaluations of each member. Among other things, this process enabled the chair to change his instruction in ways that resulted in substantially improved teaching and better course evaluations* (Pew 1992, p. 5A).

This situation probably is exceptional but demonstrates that faculty can work together to improve teaching if a commitment to do so exists. A reluctance to work collaboratively in this way contrasts markedly with prevailing practice regarding research, where it is quite common for faculty to seek advice from colleagues before submitting manuscripts for possible publication. It also is becoming increasingly common for faculty to work collaboratively on research projects that eventually lead to joint publication of the findings (Austin and Baldwin 1991).

An anecdotal record of a tenured, senior linguistics professor who collaborated with a colleague also is illustrative of what can be accomplished when teachers work together to improve teaching. In his commentary, Carton writes:

The examination of my classroom allowed me to reflect upon the degree of virtuosity and range of skills in class-room management I had acquired over the years. Whether my skills are, from a public point of view, praiseworthy is a question I had received little information about during those years in which I had hammered out some skills in almost total isolation from my peers who should perhaps have been more interested. Nor have I had the opportunity to watch enough classes of others to be able to develop some yardsticks by which to make judgments about the quality of my own classroom skills. At last, [my colleague] had led me to identify my skills and begin to make an inventory of the techniques I had at my disposal (1988, p. 58).

A finding by Baldwin may go even further, suggesting that collaboration is an indicator of vitality among faculty (1990). He notes that a substantially larger proportion of "vital" professors rather than a less capable "representative" faculty stated that they sometimes collaborate with colleagues, take professional risks, and engage in innovative or nontraditional professional activities.

Despite the complexity of and probable interactive effects between the academy's constraints and the resistance of faculty, it still is somewhat surprising that so few faculty consult with each other on teaching since, as McDaniel observes, "the most widely accepted principles of adult learning suggest that adults thrive on collaborative learning. Adults are motivated by peer involvement and support, and sharing their experiences is a powerful resource for learning" (1987, p. 94). If collaboration in teaching is to become normative rather than exceptional, ways must be found to promote such collaboration.

Rationale for Comprehensive Faculty Evaluation

Peer review may be essential if significant improvement in certain aspects of teaching is to occur (Centra 1993; Soderberg 1986). Yet, peer review is only one part of a broader process for improving this professional role. Another critical element is honest and thoughtful self-evaluation (Cross and Angelo 1988; Stevens 1988). Data provided by students, experts in specific aspects of teaching and learning, and academic administrators also may be considerably valuable. Information from various combinations of these sources can be obtained in many ways: from student ratings of courses and instructors, from interviews with students and instructors, from direct classroom observation, from videotapes and audiotapes of classes, from assessment of course materials and instructors' evaluations of the academic work of students, and from a study of other measures of student achievement (Aubrecht 1984; Menges 1991). The process should include looking at the pre-interactive (course planning and class preparation) and the post-interactive (reflection and revision) phases of teaching as well as actual delivery of instruction (Soderberg 1986).

Assessment for instructional improvement is only one purpose for which evaluation takes place. Obviously, summative evaluation is another. There very well may be other valid reasons for evaluating courses and instructors. Faculty evaluation including formative and summative components (and any other components deemed appropriate by an academic community), in which multiple constituencies are consulted and several methods and procedures are used to gather relevant data, are components of the process of comprehensive faculty evaluation.

Nearly all writers in the field of faculty evaluation recommend the adoption of comprehensive programs of faculty evaluation (Aleamoni 1981; Arden 1989; Arreola 1984; Blackburn and Clark 1975; Brandenburg, Braskamp, and Ory 1979; Centra 1979, 1993; Cohen and McKeachie 1980; Dressel 1976; Greenwood and Ramagli 1980; Romberg 1985; Sauter and Walker 1976; Schneider 1975; Scriven 1980, 1983, 1985; Seldin 1984; Smith et al. 1988; Soderberg, 1985, 1986; Spaights and Bridges 1986; Stevens and Aleamoni 1985; Study Group 1984; Swanson and Sisson 1971; Wolansky 1976). In insisting that it is critical to have a comprehensive program of evaluation, as opposed to a more limited one, in place, Dressel observes that "no one method by itself is adequate. In fact, overemphasis on one method may do more harm than good. Various facets of the program can be examined by different and appropriate means of assessment" (1976, p. 338).

Batista observes that "no technique or source of information is valid per se in evaluating college teaching. Usefulness depends on the objectives to be reached" (1976, p. 269). Likewise, Greenwood and Ramagli conclude that:

None of the means of evaluating college teaching used alone

*seems to have a research base which indicates that it is a
sufficiently valid measure of the teaching effectiveness of
a given professor. Such a situation suggests the development
of multiple data systems that are continuously validated
and subject to ongoing empirical examination of the
interrelationships existing between the different kinds of
evaluation and instructional improvement data collected*
(1980, p. 681).

However, it is not always possible for colleges and universities
to commit the necessary resources to implement all aspects
of a comprehensive program of faculty evaluation (Brandenburg, Braskamp, and Ory 1979). In this event, scholars usually
recommend that the university community ask—and answer,
after careful deliberation—three fundamental questions
before deciding what elements to implement. These questions
are: For what purpose is the evaluation being conducted?
From what sources will the information be obtained and/or
who will interpret the information gathered? What methods
and procedures will be used to gather the information? (Bulcock 1984; Cancelli 1987; Craig, Redfield, and Galluzzo 1986;
Licata 1986; Millman 1981; Prater 1983; Scriven 1980). Further,
they almost invariably emphasize that a *thoughtful* answer
to the first of these questions should precede attempts to
answer the others.

A list of questions posed by Pittman and Slate gets at some
of these same issues, but has a somewhat different focus
(1989). Their questions are: What is the overall aim of the
evaluation? What areas of faculty responsibility are to be evaluated? What are the objective limits of this evaluation? How
does one establish a framework for evaluating this/these
aim(s)? These authors say that "to omit such questions and
their consideration is likely to produce a faculty review procedure with a weak or nonexistent conceptual base. Such a system creates rather than [resolves] problems" (p. 39).

Answers to questions like these should be sought because
information from some sources and from some methods and
procedures may be relevant for one purpose, but irrelevant,
or less relevant, for another. To illustrate, several scholars (Bulcock 1984; Centra 1975; Cohen and McKeachie 1980; Scriven
1980, 1983; Sorcinelli 1984; Stodolsky 1984) argue that direct
classroom observation for summative evaluation, whether carried out by colleagues or by academic administrators, is not

normally appropriate or valid. That argument is based on low interrater reliability of observers' findings, observers' failure to make enough visits to obtain a representative sample of teaching behaviors, and the likelihood that the classroom teaching and learning environment is different when observers are present than when only students and teacher are in the room. In one experimental study, for example, researchers found that professors are much more likely to involve students in the teaching and learning process when they know observers are present than when they are unaware of the observers' presence (Ward, Clark, and Harrison 1981).

On the other hand, scholars see great potential value for classroom observation when it is used for formative evaluation. That argument is made well by Stodolsky:

In formative evaluation, direct observation may be very appropriate if too much is not made of any given observation. Direct observation can provide useful occasions for dialogue with superiors and colleagues. Specific occasions are what teaching is all about, and may provide a very appropriate focus for discussing improvement. Discussions and suggestions that follow observations of a teacher may even be more helpful if it is recognized that he or she might teach differently in different situations (1984, p. 17).

To illustrate again, Edwards (1974) and McKeachie (1986) argue that academic administrators should play a significant role in summative evaluation, where it is likely they have relevant information about all areas of professional performance, but only a supportive role in formative evaluation. These writers reason that faculty are likely to feel threatened by having administrators involved in formative evaluation, fearing that weaknesses identified in this process will be used against them later when personnel decisions are made. In formative evaluation, administrators may be better suited for behind-the-scenes roles as producers—providers of time and other resources and a generally supportive atmosphere—than as actors.

To be comprehensive, faculty evaluation must involve peer, student, and administrator evaluation and self-assessment. Not all of these constituencies figure equally for all evaluation purposes, however. Some of them may be required for all of these purposes, but others may be suitable only, or mostly,

In formative evaluation, administrators may be better suited for behind-the-scenes roles as producers than as actors.

for either formative or summative evaluation, or for some other purpose.

Comprehensive Evaluation Models

A number of conceptual models of comprehensive faculty evaluation have been developed, and every once in awhile a relatively comprehensive program has been put into place at a college or university. At this point, one of the conceptual models and a program that actually was implemented are described. After that, a program of formative evaluation of the teaching role only, based on a theory of evaluation and pilot tested in elementary schools, is described because it includes many of the elements subsequently employed at colleges and universities for evaluation of this type.

We present these models here because we are convinced that instructional improvement is contingent on information about several interdependent teaching processes, requiring input from several of the academy's constituencies. We don't want readers to think that we are under the illusion that formative peer evaluation is a "fix all" approach. Rather, we believe that the models presented will illustrate how important a comprehensive program is in improving teaching.

Soderberg model

The instructional evaluation model developed by Soderberg (1986) is three-dimensional. At every point, elements intersect so that it is virtually impossible to miss any teaching process, time phase in which an instructional event occurs, or source of information for assessing what has taken place. Figure 1 shows how the model's three dimensions are related.

The first dimension consists of a series of interdependent processes: goals and objectives (asking and answering such questions as "What are we trying to do?" and "What are our purposes at this point?"), methods and materials ("How will we go about doing what we decide to do?" and "What can we use to accomplish our goals and objectives?"), and feedback ("How will we go about finding out how we're doing?" and "How can we assess the relationship between our goals and objectives and our methods and materials?") (pp. 15-16). Answers to these questions may depend on the institution's concept of what an educated person should be, on the institution's mission, and on individual teachers' epistemological values.

FIGURE 1
Soderberg's three-dimensional model of faculty evaluation

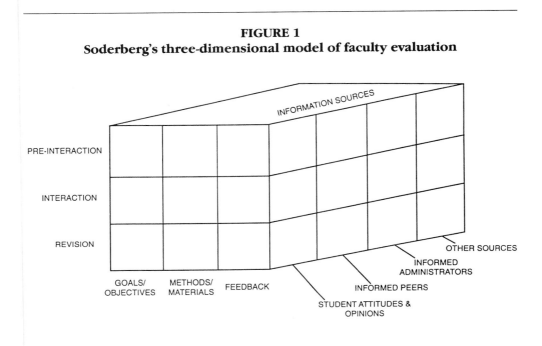

INFORMATION SOURCES

PRE-INTERACTION

INTERACTION

REVISION

OTHER SOURCES

INFORMED ADMINISTRATORS

INFORMED PEERS

GOALS/ OBJECTIVES METHODS/ MATERIALS FEEDBACK

STUDENT ATTITUDES & OPINIONS

Note: From "A Credible Model: Evaluating Classroom Teaching in Higher Education" by L.O. Soderberg, 1985. Instructional Evaluation 8(2), p. 19. Reprinted by permission.

The second dimension represents three broad time phases in which the instructional process occurs: pre-interaction (the point at which many decisions about goals and objectives, methods and materials, and feedback are made), interaction (the point at which instruction is delivered or when students are otherwise engaged in learning), and revision (the point at which reflection on and self-evaluation of events at the pre-interactive and interactive phases occur) (pp. 16-17). It has been said, though, that the most effective teachers move back and forth among phases as they plan for, modify, and monitor these events (Chenoweth 1991; Yarbrough 1987).

One classroom researcher has found that particularly successful teachers:

possessed high levels of awareness and consciousness. They were capable of meta-cognition, thinking about their thinking, or the many decisions they made before, during, and after their lessons. In effect, they were aware and immediately responsive to various student needs, concerns, and learning styles. They were quite verbal and reflective. They were able to demonstrate how they consistently took individual student needs into consideration in their planning, monitoring, and adjustments during their lessons. It was evident that they knew their students well. In addition, during the lesson, these teachers provided great clarity with lots of cues, structuring comments, advanced organizers, and the big picture for their students. They seemed determined and strong-willed about accomplishing their objectives and having students succeed.

Students were challenged and at the same time cooperative and mutually supportive of one another. Above all, these teachers were risk takers, willing to make necessary revisions and try new teaching strategies. Being open, taking chances, making immediate changes, and experimenting with new models of learning and teaching are qualities that appeared to make these teachers inspiring to both their students and the external evaluators (Chenoweth 1991, p. 303).

The third dimension of Soderberg's model is represented by the constituencies that are in a position to provide information about faculty strengths and weaknesses. Students and informed peers are seen as primary sources; informed administrators, alumni, and other sources (including self-assessment) are seen as secondary sources. Students are in a favorable position to evaluate goals and objectives, methods and materials, and feedback when these processes relate to interaction. Peers are, according to Soderberg, best equipped to assess processes related to pre-interaction and revision. The Soderberg model warrants careful study.

Romberg model
Romberg describes procedures employed in summative and formative evaluation of programs and personnel at the dental school of the University of Maryland (1985). In this program, several methods of evaluation are employed and sources consulted in five broad areas: student evaluation of instruction, including both course quality and teacher effectiveness; evaluation of the faculty for decisions regarding reappointment, promotion, and tenure; the evaluation of each department, including the formative evaluation of its goals and objectives by the faculty as well as administrators, and the formative eval-

uation of the faculty by peers and department chairpersons; faculty and student evaluation of administrators, including the dean, associate deans, and department chairpersons; and evaluation of the goals and objectives of the school by students, faculty, and administrators. The procedures include evaluation of course materials and instructors' evaluations of the academic work of students but not direct classroom observation or class videotaping.

The processes described in two of these five areas are quite conventional in that students at most colleges and universities are afforded opportunities to evaluate courses and instructors, and committees composed of faculty and administrators at most colleges and universities are asked to make recommendations concerning personnel decisions. Systematic evaluation in the remaining three areas is much less commonplace in higher education. The mechanisms that have been put into place to evaluate departmental goals and objectives and those of the school, as well as the formative evaluation of the faculty and administration by the faculty, are not employed often in colleges and universities.

Roper, Deal, and Dornbusch model

The formative evaluation of teaching model of Roper, Deal, and Dornbusch (1976) is based on the theory of evaluation of Dornbusch (1975). The model under consideration here, which was pilot tested in elementary schools, includes seven interdependent stages: identifying the participants and determining which of them will work together; defining and clarifying the teaching and learning objectives of each participant; setting the criteria by which the performance of each participant will be evaluated, based on the outlined objectives; assessing the quality of the performance of each participant through the use of direct classroom observation and often other methods; critiquing the strengths and weaknesses of the performance of each participant; communicating the results of each evaluation through direct interaction between evaluator and the faculty member whose performance is being assessed; and developing a plan for improvement based on self-assessment and student evaluation as well as on the results of the peer-review process.

Roper, Deal, and Dornbusch have recommended that the membership of each pair of participants be determined by the participants, believing that this method is preferable to random selection or arbitrary assignment. Mutual respect, trust, and compatible educational philosophies between participants, controlled by self-selection, they argue, outweigh advantages offered by other methods of selection. Agreeing that participants should determine membership of the working groups, Heller warns that attempts to impose membership could result in groups that "go through the motions" but make little legitimate attempt to improve the quality of teaching (1989).

In the Roper, Deal, and Dornbusch model and in many other formative evaluation models, participants are encouraged to identify the merit of their own objectives (either individually or collectively), to determine the methods by which data will be gathered, and to establish criteria by which strengths and weaknesses of their performance will be evaluated. Allowing participants to make these decisions is seen as a means for developing faculty ownership of the program (Heller 1989). While performance is evaluated largely by direct classroom observation, a number of methods for gathering information—including assessment of course materials, student evaluations of their teacher's effectiveness, and self-evaluation—also are important elements of the model.

After the agreed-upon methods of evaluation have been completed, the group members meet to discuss the findings. At these feedback sessions, both participants are encouraged to provide an assessment of the items under consideration. Participants have observed that criticism most often is presented as suggestions for alternative techniques, rather than as mandates or absolutes. Roper, Deal, and Dornbusch note that comments "encompassed virtually every aspect of classroom activity. Teachers learned not only about their own performance but about the overall climate of their classrooms" (p. 62).

Planning programs for improvement evolve from the feedback sessions, from student evaluation, and from self-reflection on performance in general. At these improvement-planning sessions, participants work collaboratively to determine the strategies that might be employed in efforts to improve performance, the resources that may be required to accomplish these objectives, and the means by which these instructional-improvement efforts will be evaluated.

Roper, Deal, and Dornbusch report that participants were enthusiastic about the program and that many of them planned to continue to work with colleagues in programs like this one in the future. There is no indication, though, that the program has been widely adopted by elementary or secondary schools or by colleges and universities. However, elements of it have been used in the isolated formative peer-evaluation programs that have been identified. In later sections of this report (Incentives and Disincentives), ways that may make programs of this type more appealing to faculty and that may discourage them from participating, respectively, will be addressed.

Faculty Roles In Formative Evaluation

It is difficult to quarrel with Batista's conclusion that "colleague evaluation is better used when the categories are those in which faculty members are in the better position to cast judgments than anyone else" (1976, pp. 269-70). The same might be said of students, teaching consultants, administrators, and others who supply information about teaching performance. It also should be emphasized again that assessments of teaching by any of these sources "are not necessarily valid indicators of effective teaching when used by themselves, but they may be helpful when used in conjunction with other evidence" (Cohen and McKeachie 1980, p. 147).

The conceptual model of Soderberg is instructive in identifying areas in which peer review, as well as evaluation by other constituencies, are most appropriate (1986). In this model, teaching processes (setting of goals and objectives, determining what methods and materials will be used in teaching, and providing feedback) interact with the time phases (pre-interaction, interaction, and revision) at which instructional decisions and actions occur and with the constituencies (faculty, students, academic administrators, and others) that could provide relevant information about teacher performance.

Soderberg suggests that faculty colleagues are best qualified to assess processes occurring at the pre-interactive and revision phases (1986). Cohen and McKeachie (1980) and Seldin (1984) envision an even broader role for colleagues, including assessment of what occurs during delivery of instruction (and when students are otherwise engaged in learning) as well as what occurs before and after. Hart advocates a particularly prominent role for faculty as classroom observers, noting that faculty have expertise about teaching and learning that students simply aren't in a position to possess (1987). Katz and Henry also recommend classroom observation by colleagues and suggest that it be combined with interviews of selected students (1988).

In this section, we examine a range of roles that scholars suggest as appropriate for faculty to play in formative evaluation. We cite primarily the writings of Batista (1976), Cohen and McKeachie (1980), Hart (1987), Scriven (1985, 1987), and Soderberg (1986) but refer also to the scholarship of other writers on specific aspects of evaluation. We also look briefly at the potential and limitations of students, teaching consultants, and academic administrators in the process of

The conceptual model of Soderberg is instructive in identifying areas in which peer review, as well as evaluation by other constituencies, are most appropriate.

teaching improvement.

Faculty Roles

Cohen and Mckeachie provide a useful classification of roles that faculty could play in evaluating colleagues' teaching (1980). The categories of this classification are: elements of course design, including goals, course content, and organization; methods and materials employed in delivery of instruction; evaluation of students and grading practices; and integration and interpretation of information gathered from students, administrators, and self-evaluation as well as evaluation by peers.

There is considerable overlap between this classification and Scriven's listing of criteria on which teaching evaluation should be based (1985). These criteria are:

> *The quality of the content taught (does the teacher really know the subject well enough to provide sound and illuminating answers to any questions that the best student could legitimately ask about the actual or required curriculum content); the success in imparting and/or inspiring learning (which includes learning the value of learning, of systematic inquiry, cooperation, etc.—that is, learning is not restricted to the cognitive domain); the mastery of professional skills (how to set valid tests, deal with the nonclassroom duties, etc.); and the adherence to ethical standards (avoiding racism and favoritism, etc.)* (p. 36).

Elaborating on these criteria, Scriven develops especially the second one, noting that faculty have responsibility in "increasing the amount of valuable learning acquired by the students, . . . increasing their capacity for learning" (1987, p. 10), and "increasing [their] learning to something like the level at which the students are capable" (p. 21).

Scriven does not address the issue of how success (or failure) in meeting these criteria are to be determined, except for insisting that specialists take a look at tests written by faculty and the grading of these tests (1985, 1987). Fellow faculty may be in a particularly favorable position to evaluate aspects of all of these criteria, as Cohen and McKeachie suggest (1980).

Elements of course design

In the category of course design, Cohen and McKeachie suggest that faculty colleagues examine the following:

- The professor's mastery of course content.
- Appropriateness of course objectives.
- Selection of course content (knowledge of what must be taught).
- Organization of the course.
- Coverage of appropriate content.
- Incorporation of recent scholarship into selection of content.
- Suitability of student assignments in meeting course objectives.

In this same general area, Soderberg suggests that informed peers assess the suitability of objectives for particular groups of students and the appropriateness of the rigor of the course in its contextual environment (1986).

Instructional methods and materials

In the category of instructional methods and materials, Cohen and McKeachie cite five areas in which colleagues could assess the effectiveness of fellow faculty: suitability of methods of instruction in meeting course goals; appropriateness of the reading list for the course; reasonableness of the amount of time required of students for completing readings, written assignments, and other projects; appropriateness of handouts and other instructional materials in facilitating learning; and suitability of various types of media in meeting course objectives. Batista includes a related item: the application of appropriate methodologies for teaching specific content (1976).

Evaluation of the academic work of students

In assessing the devices employed by professors for evaluating student assignments and their grading practices, Cohen and McKeachie recommend that colleagues examine:

- The length and difficulty of examinations.
- The coverage given to higher-order, as well as lower-level, cognitive processes on examinations and on other assignments.

- The time and effort required of students to complete written assignments and other projects.
- The specificity by which grading practices are explained to students.

Soderberg recommends three additional competencies in this area that faculty could critique: the relationship of evaluation instruments to course objectives and procedures, the usefulness of the evaluation to students in the learning process, and the relationship between awarding of course grades and the grading system communicated to students (1986).

Scriven emphasizes the importance of two related items: test construction and the grading of student examinations. In suggesting that faculty with expertise in tests and measurements assess the competence of colleagues in these areas, he observes that "few teachers, from kindergarten to postgraduate, have ever had their tests and scoring keys looked at against minimum standards of professional competence, if indeed they have ever heard of such standards; and those that have been looked at present a very depressing picture" (1985, p. 32).

The professional competence to which Scriven refers is related to recommendations that experts check to see that professors grade essay tests: "blind," so that biases for and against students are minimized; question by question, rather than test by test, so as to reduce potential "halo effects" and to maintain uniform standards of evaluation from the first answer read to the last; and in random order ("shuffling" the papers after reading answers to each question) so that reader enthusiasm, frustration, and fatigue affect students in no predetermined way. An alternative argument may be made that it is advantageous to know the name associated with the work. In this scenario, the instructor can bring to the evaluation an understanding of the student's prior knowledge and unique background and perspectives. This may shed light upon a student's response that might be lost in blind review. Experts in tests and measurements can also be considerably helpful to colleagues in the construction of "objective" tests, where writing good questions often proves difficult.

Integration and interpretation
Cohen and McKeachie indicate that colleagues are ideally equipped to integrate and interpret information gathered from

various methods of evaluation and from all sources providing information. In the evaluation of instruction, they suggest that peers assess the following: student ratings in light of circumstances under which the course was taught (e.g., large vs. small enrollment in classes, required vs. elective course, and a number of other contingencies that can affect student ratings); the criteria used in evaluation instruction; and the weighing of the criteria used in determining teaching effectiveness.

Batista lists a number of other factors that could be considered by colleagues in the integrative stage of instructional evaluation:

1. Faculty members' own evaluations of their teaching.
2. Faculty members' own evaluation of their knowledge of specific content areas within the field as a whole.
3. Informal course evaluations conducted by instructors with their students.
4. Alumni ratings of faculty members.
5. Student achievement in courses.
6. Interviews with groups of students or individual students (1976).

Craig, Redfield, and Galluzzo (1986) and McKeachie (1986) recommend that the integrative process also include a study of the relationship between students' explanations of their responsibility in teaching and learning and their evaluations of courses and instructors. These researchers are convinced that information provided by such comparisons would be a valuable tool in assessing both quality of teaching and student learning.

While integrating and interpreting information appear to be important, they must not be considered faculty's only responsibility. If faculty are not willing to examine aspects of teaching they are uniquely qualified to assess, there is that danger that:

> What is 'peer reviewed' is not the process of teaching and its products (the learning that the teaching enabled) but [merely] the observations and ratings submitted by students and assorted others. This situation is in part a function of faculty uneasiness about the instruction of colleagues in their classrooms. But underneath this uneasiness lies a more troubling circumstance: the lack of clarity about why faculty

should *be observers of one another's teaching [emphasis theirs]* (Edgerton, Hutchings, and Quinlan 1991, p. 5).

Clearly, these scholars believe that faculty must become involved in assessing several aspects of colleagues' teaching, and that this involvement should extend beyond an integrative function.

Peer observation

While Cohen and McKeachie acknowledge a need for formative peer observation, their classification deals with this method only implicitly. Other scholars provide more detail on how peer observation could be employed.

Hart, believing that faculty should play a broad role in instructional improvement, identifies events that occur during delivery that faculty are especially well-qualified to assess (1987). These events are: the place where and the time when classes are taught and other physical factors affecting delivery of instruction; the procedures used by the teachers in conducting the class; the teacher's use of language to inform, explain, persuade, and motivate, and the language students use in responding and reacting to the teacher; the roles played by teachers and students as they interact; the relationship of what is occurring in a particular class to other courses, disciplines, and the curriculum in general; and the outcomes of teaching, as reflected in student learning. These roles are discussed in more detail in the next section of the report, where the place of direct classroom observation is specifically addressed.

Recognizing that faculty have the potential to contribute to teaching improvement of colleagues in several significant ways, Seldin (1984) fills in and expands on areas in which other scholars have agreed that faculty have expertise. The following questions framed by Seldin could be used by faculty as they assess colleagues' performance.

We believe that scholars have demonstrated, rather convincingly, that competent faculty can critique colleagues' teaching and assist their peers in improving that teaching. Several methods are available for doing so.

Roles for Constituencies Other Than the Faculty

In the remainder of this section, we look briefly at some of the strengths and limitations of students, academic administrators, and teaching consultants as providers of information in formative evaluation of teaching. We make no attempt to be comprehensive but hope to show instead that each constituency can contribute relevant data, though none of them can provide all the information needed by professors who wish to improve their teaching.

Students

Students evaluate college teachers and courses more than any other constituency (Bergman 1980; Seldin 1984). They are relied upon not only because it is relatively easy to devise teacher-rating forms, administer the forms, and tabulate the results (Abrami 1985) but also because, as Cross and Angelo say, "students have ample opportunity to see teachers in action in good days and bad, [and] they are in a good position to evaluate the impact of the teaching on themselves as learners" (1988, p. 125). It is difficult to deny that students are in a position to provide reliable information about certain types of teacher behaviors.

Students probably are most qualified to evaluate aspects of teacher performance occurring at the delivery phase of the instructional process (Soderberg 1986). They seem less qualified—even unqualified—to assess many aspects of performance occurring at the pre-interactive and revision phases, except for how delivery is impacted by events occurring at other times.

When completing teacher rating forms, students usually are asked to assess several elements: style characteristics associated with delivery (class preparation, organization, sense of humor, enthusiasm, rapport with students, etc., called "observables" by Bulcock [1984] and "secondary indicators" by Scriven [1987]); their perceptions of what they have learned and of the instructor's command of the subject matter; and overall impressions of the quality of the instructor's teaching and the course. Some of the information they provide probably is necessary for summative evaluation (for example, global ratings of the teacher and course). Other information may be useful in formative evaluation. Some of it may be invalid for either purpose. Students, like every other constituency, have strengths and limitations in the faculty-evaluation process.

To determine what students are, and are not, in a favorable position to evaluate, it may be instructive to look again at the criteria on which faculty evaluation should be based. According to Scriven, there are but four such criteria: quality of content taught, the instructor's success in teaching that content and in inspiring learning, the instructor's mastery of professional skills in writing tests and evaluating the academic work of students, and the instructor's adherence to ethical standards (1985). Students appear qualified, as observers of classroom—and certain out-of-class—proceedings, to assess the instructor's success in organizing and delivering the course content and inspiring learning, and the instructor's adherence to ethical standards associated with teaching, although other constituencies also are in a favorable position to comment on these factors. Except in the most egregious instances, where faculty are clearly incompetent in knowledge of subject matter, for example, faculty and academic administrators are in a considerably better position than students to evaluate the quality of the content taught and, with the help of experts in tests and measurements, the tests written by teachers and the quality of the academic work submitted by students. Students too often are asked to evaluate much that lies outside of their areas of expertise.

Except for some possible connection to "success in imparting and/or inspiring learning," the style characteristics that teachers exhibit as they deliver instruction are not related directly to Scriven's criteria (1985). And even with that dimension, there may be better indicators than the style characteristics. Yet, as Scriven suggests, such "secondary indicators" may have:

> a useful role in formative evaluation as follows. If you have demonstrated that a teacher is doing badly, using the proper criteria, then the "anthology of successful styles" built up by researchers provides a valuable resource for suggestions as to practices the teacher might consider adding to his or her current repertoire in the quest for improvement (1987, p. 37).

The validity of student ratings may be called into question in a number of other ways, as Abrami (1985) and others have suggested, when:

1. Teacher rating forms include a disproportionately larger number of items on "success in imparting and/or inspiring learning," as Scriven (1987) phrases it, and a dispro-

portionately smaller number of items on other valid evaluation criteria;

2. The forms include greater numbers of items on interaction
between students and instructor and fewer on important
aspects of teaching that occur during pre-interaction and
feedback phases of the instructional process;

3. Forms include items appropriate for some classes, academic disciplines, styles of teaching, and teaching methodologies but less appropriate (or inappropriate) for others; for example, the forms may be better suited to the
social sciences than the humanities; and

4. A student's response to one item affects responses to other
items, a threat to validity called the "halo effect"; this
effect may bias results either for or against a teacher.

Abrami also notes that:

> Students as a group may be inaccurate observers for a va-
> riety of reasons: they may be naive and insensitive to qual-
> itative differences in instruction; they may be collectively
> biased by their own expectations which distort their percep-
> tions; [and] they may be unfairly lenient in judging teach-
> ing effectiveness (1985, p. 217).

While information provided by students via teacher rating
forms can contribute to an understanding of teacher performance, the picture they paint often is incomplete. More detail
can be filled in when this information is augmented by data
gathered from other sources, including the faculty.

Academic administrators

Because academic administrators usually were faculty members before assuming their present positions, or continue to
teach as administrators, they, like faculty, have expertise about
teaching and learning, teacher performance, concern about
colleagues' teaching, etc., that students don't have. They are
in a good position to evaluate aspects of teaching that occur
at the pre-interactive and feedback phases of instruction as
well as when instruction actually takes place. Like faculty and
teaching consultants, they should be able to assess quality
of content taught, the instructor's success in assessing student
work and in inspiring learning, and the procedures employed
in teaching content. But administrators are further removed
from the faculty than their colleagues.

Since much of an administrator's time is consumed by responsibilities other than teaching, administrators are less likely to interact with faculty to the same degree and in the same ways as fellow faculty. There also is the likelihood that faculty will be reluctant to seek help from administrators in improving their teaching, believing that deficiencies in performance will be used against them when personnel decisions are made. These factors may limit the effectiveness of administrators in a process aimed at instructional improvement.

Teaching consultants and faculty development programs

Teaching consultants normally offer assistance to faculty in one or more of the following broad areas: instructional development, personal development, and institutional development (Bergquist and Phillips 1975). The type of programming offered depends in part on the philosophies of the consultant and of the institution's administrators, and on time and other available resources. Interest in faculty development has waxed and waned from the time the first programs were put in place in the early 1970s, but considerable interest in them has been shown in recent years.

Teaching consultants usually have expertise in a number of teaching areas: strategies, student learning, learning styles, and technology. There is little doubt they can be catalysts for improved teaching among faculty who are motivated to work with them.

Mathis, in observing that many faculty development officers are psychologists by training, concludes that:

> *Those who organize institutional programs for instructional development should be aware of the 'culture' of the many disciplines in higher education. While psychology may have much to say about teaching and learning, psychologists are not always able to communicate this to their colleagues outside of psychology in a language easily accepted or understood. The value of having faculty in the many fields of study who know the research literature on teaching and learning, and who can communicate with their colleagues in the language of their discipline, suggests that instructional development can best be served by preparing faculty to perform an instructional development function in their own field rather than anticipating salvation from a central hive populated with psychologists* (1974, pp. 10-11).

This admonition suggests that there should be a close connection between the instructional improvement side of faculty development and formative peer evaluation.

Despite being written about 20 years ago, Mathis's advice regarding faculty development centers seems as relevant now as it probably was then:

> *The Center approach is successful only to the degree that Center programs and staff are responsive to the diverse, and sometimes conflicting, needs of the campus. Centers should not staff themselves to reflect any one orthodoxy about teaching. The successful Center should be able to assist the faculty member who is looking for a teaching system to the same degree that it can help a faculty member with sympathetic advice. [Such Centers] ought to avoid academic evangelism as much as possible. The temptation to save the natives from themselves through an aggressive program of prophylaxis, usually technological in nature, is generally nonproductive, since it involves programs for the few at the expense of the many. The natives should save themselves, and Centers should be as eclectic as possible in helping them do so* (1974, p. 25).

Although ultimately sustained by a personal desire to succeed, buoyed no doubt by mastery of and passion for a field of study, good teaching is most likely to occur in a culture where teaching is valued and where there is a support system in place that encourages its development. The commitment of administrators is essential. While the support of all segments of the academic community is important, the faculty have a key role because they can look at what takes place in classrooms and beyond from different perspectives than students, in more detail than administrators, and perhaps in ways that command more confidence and trust from faculty than either teaching consultants or administrators. Colleagues, using a variety of methods, can look at what their peers do and why they do it within context of their academic disciplines.

In the next section, we look at five of these methods: direct classroom observation, videotaping of classes, assessment of course materials, evaluation of instructor evaluations of the academic work of students, and analysis of teaching portfolios.

METHODS OF FORMATIVE EVALUATION

It seems clear that faculty are well-qualified to assess many aspects of colleagues' teaching and related professional activities and some of the effects of that teaching on student learning. Because faculty expertise about teaching and student learning, and their knowledge of colleagues' performance, are acquired in several ways, a number of methods of evaluation, used in combination rather than independently, are helpful to gain insight into an instructor's role in the teaching-learning process and to determine how teaching might be improved. Fellow faculty can look at some of what peers do prior to interacting with students (or before students are otherwise engaged in study), at what occurs when a teacher and students interact, and at how a teacher evaluates his or her performance with respect to student learning. They also can examine the complex relationships among the following variables: goals, objectives, and course planning; methods, materials, and procedures; and the feedback students receive from teachers and the teacher's assessment of student learning.

A number of scholars believe that peer observation is essential if the evaluation is for instructional improvement.

Five methods that have been used by colleagues to assess their peers' teaching for the purpose of instructional improvement are: direct classroom observation, videotaping of classes, evaluation of course materials, assessment of instructor evaluations of student academic work, and analysis of teaching portfolios. The merits and limitations of the first four of these methods, and what can—and cannot—be learned from and how to use each of them, are examined in detail in this section. Also examined, though in somewhat briefer form, is the role of the teaching portfolio in instructional improvement.

Direct Classroom Observation

While most scholars express serious reservations about the use of direct classroom observation in summative evaluation, nearly all of them agree that it can be employed effectively in formative evaluation. A number of scholars believe that peer observation is essential if the evaluation is for instructional improvement.

Objectives

Scholars argue that peer observation should be employed because faculty members have expertise in the process of teaching and learning that is not possessed to the same degree by either students or administrators (Braskamp 1978; Centra 1986, 1993; Cohen and McKeachie 1980; Shulman 1993;

Soderberg 1986; Sorcinelli 1984). Some of them also suggest that it is a vital component of the process, because it is the only way in which some aspects of teaching can be assessed adequately.

In regard to improving the quality of instruction through classroom observation, Hart observes:

To improve, teachers need the help and support of other teachers. Teachers need to consult regularly, over an extended period, with other teachers. Teachers need to observe other teachers at work, be observed by them in return, and share their observations, reflections, and recommendations (1987, p. 15).

While acknowledging a practical problem associated with classroom observation, Weimer, like Hart, stresses some of its important benefits:

[Faculty] need to be in each other's classes regularly, routinely. To expect that to occur may be naive and unrealistic. Faculty labor under multiple demands. Nevertheless, observations . . . should not be special, one-time activity. They need to be an ongoing part of teaching. They keep instructors fresh, encourage and develop accurate self-assessment, and make obvious the complexities of the teaching-learning phenomenon (1990, p. 122).

But it should be emphasized that direct classroom observation may not be "easy, comfortable, simple, or quick in results" (Hart 1987, p. 15).

While several programs in which peers have observed a colleague's classroom have been presented in the literature (some of them will be described in the next section), much less has been written about the specific events that might be observed. A particularly cogent discussion of six interrelated categories of these events is provided by Hart.

1. The physical-temporal setting. Hart notes that the:

time of day, room size and shape, air (or the lack of it), light (or dark), surrounding noise, furnishings, apparatus, and clutter [affect] how the people of the event use or misuse this environment: their uses of space, access, positioning,

*distance, mobilities. . . . [While] the teacher may need few
reminders of the ecology, the reactions of the observer may
well help to understand and use it better* (pp. 17-18).

2. Classroom structure and procedures. Hart observes that
   each class has:

*its intellectual structures, orders, sequences, its texture of
governing ideas, its proportions, connections, transitions,
planned or not. Some teachers regularly signal to the class
what these are, others (ill-advisedly, I think) take them for
granted. Teaching is, among other things, a composing process. . . . The observer can, at least, keep track of the structures or logics that are communicated, and report them
back—occasionally to the teacher's surprise* (p. 18).

3. The rhetorical dimension. Hart notes that certain types
   and levels of language are employed by teachers and students and concludes that:

*they are sometimes similar, sometimes quite distinct—even
separate or divisive. . . . But not many teachers in my experience are aware of the languages they use. The observer
can hear and report the relative degrees of difficulty, for-
mality, technicality, the dominant syntactic forms. . . . Every
class session has its rhetoric: certain forms and methods that
are used to achieve certain ends—informative, explanatory,
persuasive. . . . To carry out these complex aims, the teacher
uses certain tactics and methods: assignments, exercises,
demonstrations, examples, analogies, and motivational
appeals. The observer can learn to observe and report the
ends and the appropriateness of the means* (p. 18).

4. The dramaturgical-sociopolitical dimension. Hart observes:

*We are all sufficiently familiar with dramaturgy to be use-
ful observers of how members of a class play their roles and
how they interact. We can record such phenomena as pa-
cing, voicing, nonverbal behavior and communication, the
class dynamic, its degree of intensity and involvement. . . .
We can observe how the teacher uses authority (or power)
and what kinds, interpret the politics of the class, the directions and commands, invitations, judgments, rewards, and
threats* (p. 19).

5. The curricular context. While the curricular context probably cannot be directly observed, an observer can make certain inferences about the class's relationship to:

larger designs, other courses and areas of study, other disciplines, levels of learning and development, academic goals and values, extramural preoccupations and influences. No class is an island. What uses are *made of such foreign relations, and how many, can be observed. What uses and how many* should *be made is a legitimate issue of strategy and priority* (p. 19).

6. The effects of teaching. Hart stresses that the outcomes of teaching are what really matter, but notes:

Most teachers unwittingly cling to the assumption that time needed for teaching leaves no time in class for finding out what is being learned. . . . The observer can only try to catch the clues and report them, and try to help the teacher find and use more adequate ways of discovering what has been learned (p. 19).

Hart's classification may seem imposing, even overwhelming, to faculty who have not been involved before in classroom observation. In program planning, the guidelines might be used as a conceptual tool to define what might be accomplished. Later, after classroom observation has been put into place, observers might use the guidelines to focus on specific aspects, but not necessarily all aspects, of teaching.

Peer observation models

Most programs of classroom observation in higher education are based on a model described by Bergquist and Phillips (1975) or on clinical supervision models employed in elementary and secondary schools. The Bergquist and Phillips model has three interdependent stages: contracting, information collection and analysis, and information feedback.

In the contracting stage, "the instructor should determine what type of information concerning his teaching he wishes to receive" (p. 88), and he or she and the observer(s) should agree on the procedures to be used in assessing the instructor's teaching. These procedures may include, for example, videotaping and interviewing students as well as classroom observation. Information collection and analysis is the stage in which observation and other agreed-upon data-gathering procedures and systematic data analysis occur. Collection of data should be carefully orchestrated, with analysis confined to areas of teaching in which the course instructor seeks assistance. The information-feedback stage usually involves two events: a brief written report in which major conclusions are outlined and a meeting in which the instructor and observer(s) discuss findings and recommendations.

The type of peer observation proposed by Sorcinelli (1984) is like the clinical supervision models (e.g., Goldhammer 1969) in that the process involves pre-observation, observation, and post-observation phases. The questions she suggests be asked during each phase (Figures 2, 3, and 4) could be particularly useful to faculty with limited experience observing colleagues' classes. Despite being designed expressly for peer observation, colleague observers also must be familiar with a peer's course materials, since the observer sometimes is asked to compare what is occurring in a colleague's class to information contained in his or her course materials. Observers using Sorcinelli's guidelines may need to be cautioned not to place too much emphasis on teaching strategies and delivery skills and not to neglect the faculty member's content knowledge and ability to communicate it effectively to students.

FIGURE 2

Pre-Observation Conference Guide

1. Briefly, what will be happening in the class I will observe?
2. What is your goal for the class? What do you hope students will gain from this session?
3. What do you expect students to do in the class to reach stated goals?
4. What can I expect you to do in class? What role will you take? What teaching methods will you use?
5. What have students been asked to do to prepare for this class?
6. What was done in earlier classes to lead up to this one?
7. Will this class be generally typical of your teaching? If not, what will be different?
8. Is there anything specific on which you would like me to focus during this class?

Note. From "An Approach to Colleague Evaluation of Classroom Instruction" by M.D. Sorcinelli, 1984. *Journal of Instructional Development* 7 (4), p. 14. Reprinted by permission.

FIGURE 3

Classroom Observation Guide

Students' and Teacher's Attitudes and Behaviors Before Class Begins
1. Do students arrive noticeably early or late?
2. Do they talk to each other?
3. Do they prepare for class? Take out books and notebooks?
4. When does the instructor arrive?
5. What does he or she do before class (write on board, encourage informal discussion with students, sit behind the desk)?

Teacher's Knowledge of Subject Matter
1. Does the instructor exhibit knowledge and mastery of the content?
2. Is the depth and breadth of material covered appropriate to the level of the course and this group of students?
3. Does the material covered relate to the syllabus and goals of the course?
4. Does the instructor present the origin of ideas and concepts?
5. Does he or she contrast the implications of various theories?
6. Does he or she emphasize a conceptual grasp of the material?
7. Does he or she present recent developments in the discipline?
8. Does he or she present divergent points of view?
9. Is there too much or not enough material included in the class session?
10. Is the content presented considered important within the discipline or within related disciplines?

Teacher's Organization and Presentation Skills
A. *Engaging Student Interest*
1. Does the instructor prepare students for the learning that is to follow by assessing what they know about the topic through use of analogy, a thought-provoking question, reference to a common experience, etc.?

B. *Introduction*
1. Does the instructor provide an overview of the class objectives?
2. Does he or she relate the day's lesson to previous class sessions?
3. Does he or she use an outline on the board or overhead projector?

C. *Organization and Clarity*
1. Is the sequence of covered content logical?
2. Is the instructor able to present content in a clear and logical manner that is made explicit to students?
3. Does he or she provide transitions from topic to topic, make distinctions between major and minor points, and periodically summarize the most important ideas?

4. Does he or she define new concepts and terms?
5. Does he or she use illustrations and examples to clarify difficult ideas?
6. Does he or she use relevant examples to explain major points?
7. Does he or she provide handouts when appropriate?

D. Teaching Strategies
1. Are the instructor's teaching methods appropriate for the goals of the class?
2. Is he or she able to vary the pattern of instruction through movement around the class, gestures, voice level, tone, and pace?
3. Does, or could, he or she use alternative methods such as media, discussion, lectures, questions, case studies, etc.?
4. Is the use of the chalkboard effective? Is the board work legible, organized?
5. If appropriate, does he or she use students' work (writing assignments, homework assignments, etc.)?
6. Are the various teaching strategies effectively integrated?

E. Closure
1. Does the instructor summarize and integrate major points of the class session at the end of the period?
2. Does he or she relate the class session to upcoming class sessions or topics?
3. Are assignments presented clearly? Hurriedly or drawn out?
4. Are assignments appropriate to class goals and course level?
5. Are students attentive until the class session ends? Or are they restless (talking, closing notebooks, etc.) before the class ends?
6. What happens after class? Are there informal discussions among students or between the instructor and students after class?

Teacher's Discussion and Questioning Skills
A. Introduction to Discussion
1. How is discussion initiated?
2. Are the purposes and guidelines clear to students?
3. Does the instructor encourage student involvement?

B. Types of Questions
1. Are questions rhetorical or real? One at a time or multiple?
2. Does the instructor use centering questions (to refocus students' attention on a particular topic), probing questions (to require students to go beyond a superficial or incomplete answer), or redirecting questions (to ask for clarification or agreement from others in the class)?

C. Level of Questions
1. What level of questions does the instructor ask? (Lower-level ques-

tions usually have a fixed or "right" answer and require students to recall, list, or define principles or facts. Higher-level questions ask students to generalize, compare, contrast, analyze, or synthesize information in meaningful patterns.)

D. What Is Done with Student Questions
1. Are questions answered in a direct and understandable manner?
2. Are questions answered politely and enthusiastically?

E. What Is Done with Student Responses
1. How long does the instructor pause for student responses (formulating answers to difficult questions takes a few minutes)?
2. Does he or she use verbal reinforcement?
3. Does he or she use nonverbal responses (e.g., smile, nod, puzzled look)?
4. Does he or she repeat answers when necessary so the entire class can hear?
5. Is he or she receptive to student suggestions or viewpoints contrary to his or her own?

Teacher's Presentation Styles
A. Verbal Communications
1. Can the instructor's voice be clearly heard?
2. Does he or she raise or lower voice for variety and emphasis?
3. Is the rate of speech appropriate? Too fast or too slow? Appropriate for note taking?
4. Are speech fillers (e.g., "you know" or "in fact") distracting?
5. Does the instructor talk to the class, not to chalkboard or ceiling?

B. Nonverbal Communication
1. Does the instructor look directly at students?
2. Does he or she scan the class when asking or responding to questions?
3. Does he or she focus on particular students or sides of the room?
4. Do facial and body movements contradict speech or expressed intentions?
5. Does the instructor use facial expressions (such as raised eyebrows), body posture (sitting, standing, folding arms), or body motions (proximity to students, clenched fists, pointing) to sustain student interest?

Students' Behaviors
1. What are the note taking patterns in the class (do students take few notes, write down everything, write down what instructor puts on the board, lean over to copy others' notes in order to keep up)?

2. Are students listening attentively, leaning forward, slumped back in desks, heads on hands?
3. Do students listen or talk when other students or the instructor are involved in discussion?
4. How actively are students involved (asking questions, doing homework, doodling on notebooks, looking out the window)?
5. Are there behaviors that are out of the mainstream of class activity (random conversations among students, reading materials not relevant to class, passing notes)?

Note. Adapted from "An Approach to Colleague Evaluation of Classroom Instruction" by M.D. Sorcinelli, 1984. *Journal of Instructional Development* 7(4), pp. 14-16. Used by permission.

FIGURE 4

Post-Observation Conference Guide

1. In general, how do you think the class went?
2. What do you think about your teaching during the class?
3. Did students accomplish the goals you had planned for the class?
4. Is there anything that worked well for you in class today—that you particularly liked? Does it usually go well?
5. Is there anything that did not work well—that you disliked about the way the class went? Is this typically a problem area for you?
6. What were your teaching strengths? Did you notice anything you improved or any personal goals you met?
7. What were your teaching problems—areas that still need improvement?
8. Do you have any suggestions or strategies for improvement?

Note. Adapted from "An Approach to Colleague Evaluation of Classroom Instruction" by M.D. Sorcinelli, 1984. *Journal of Instructional Development* 7(4), p. 16. Reprinted by permission.

Selection of observers

Whether collaborators—teacher and one or more observers— come from the same, related, or different disciplines probably depends on several factors, including: the purpose for which the assessment is conducted, participants' expectations from the observation process, specific aspects of teaching faculty seek to improve, and each teacher's comfort level with different collaborative arrangements. It may be that all of these arrangements have something to offer when the purpose of evaluation is instructional improvement, but there is far from full agreement on this issue.

Scriven (1980), Mathias and Rutherford (1982a, 1982b), Shulman (1993), and Sorcinelli (1984) adamantly argue that colleagues familiar with course content should assess a peer's teaching, because it is in course content that faculty have more expertise than students, academic administrators, and teaching consultants. That view is expressed by Sorcinelli:

> *Put simply, a colleague from one's own or a related department is in the most advantageous position to observe and evaluate aspects of the instructor's mastery and selection of course content as well as the currency or importance of that content within the discipline. Judgments about issues such as exhibited knowledge of the content, and presentation of the origin of ideas and concepts, current developments in the field, and the appropriate depth and breadth of material cannot be judged adequately by observers with limited or no content expertise. It is these tough but important criteria that classroom visitation programs need to address* (1984, p. 12).

Other scholars either believe there are advantages in having observers from nonrelated fields of study (Heller 1989; Menges 1987; Shatzky and Silberman 1986) or suggest there is a place for observers from the same and different disciplines (Braskamp 1978; Weimer 1990; Weimer, Kerns, and Parrett 1988). The first of these views is argued by Menges:

> *When feedback deals with [how content is presented], a colleague's detailed knowledge of course content may hinder rather than help. Conversations tend to focus on substantive details which are less pertinent than data about teacher or student behavior. One task of colleague observers is to take the role of naive learner, but it is even more difficult for a colleague from the same discipline to assume that role than it is for one from a distant discipline* (1987, p. 86).

In that connection, Weimer, Kerns, and Parrett add:

> *There are some arguments in favour of colleague observers from outside the discipline. Those familiar with the content over-emphasise it in relation to the rest of the instructional*

*event. If the content is unfamiliar, the observer tends toward
the opposite extreme and consequently focuses more easily
on presentational strategies and techniques. To say colleague
observers are totally unqualified because they do not know
the discipline denies the validity of their long experience as
students and instructors. They know what it is like to take
courses outside one's academic area. This means they can
reminisce and project. "If I were a student in this course,
I think that so many required readings would dampen my
enthusiasm"* (1988, p. 288).

Weimer, in qualifying that view, at least to a degree, contends:

*In some situations, [having observers from the same dis-
cipline] does help. When knowledge of the content makes
a contribution to improvement efforts, it is knowledge of
the material from a general rather than specific perspective.
. . . The way content is "shaped and ordered" by the various
disciplines does have instructional implications, and colleague understanding of those content configurations can
contribute to certain kinds of instructional decisions* (1990,
p. 118).

There may be practical reasons as well for having outside
observers, as Weimer notes:

*Pairing faculty across departments reduces anxiety and
helps to ensure that the focus is on teaching processes as
opposed to content. Confidentiality is also easier to protect
if the colleague is from across campus, not just down the
hall. Moreover, not knowing the content encourages the colleague to view the instruction from that very important student perspective. "How would I be responding if I were
required to take this class? When was I clear/confused
about the content? When did I find my attention waning?"*
(1990, p. 119)

Using observers from different academic disciplines may also
eliminate, or at least reduce, potential conflicts of interest aris-
ing from having the same faculty involved in both summative
and formative evaluation. It might also be possible to have
lower-level courses observed by colleagues from different
fields of study and upper-level courses by faculty from the

*In order to be
reliable and
valid, the
number of
classroom
observations
must be
sufficient to
assure that an
instructor's
typical
teaching has
been sampled.*

same discipline.

When evaluation is conducted for the purpose of instructional improvement, Weimer, Kerns, and Parrett recommend:

> *If the colleague observer is to acquire data related to course content, its propriety, currency, level of complexity, etc., then the observer must be familiar with the content. If the interest is more presentational, instructor enthusiasm, organisation, impartiality, etc., then the peer observer must be trained in observational techniques but familiarity with the content is not required* (1988, p. 288).

We take essentially the same view, finding it consistent, for the most part, with Shulman's "knowledge and teaching" construct (1987). We recommend, then, that reviewers come from different disciplines when faculty seek to improve presentational skills, but from the same or a closely related discipline when faculty want to strengthen aspects of teaching related to course content. Despite a certain surface attractiveness for, and perhaps expediency of, routinely selecting peer observers from nonrelated fields of study, we believe that the vast majority of critical teaching incidents are interdependently content- and context-bound, requiring analysis from and the assistance of colleagues with considerable expertise in the field of study. To work successfully, we caution, such an arrangement mandates "good faith" efforts from participants. We are confident that faculty can, and will, work in a spirit of magnanimity to improve each other's teaching and to elevate the role of instruction to its rightful lofty position in the academy.

Procedures

Two other, related procedural issues should be considered. The first is how often colleagues should visit another faculty member's class. The second is how long a collaborative relationship should continue.

In order to be reliable and valid, the number of classroom observations must be sufficient to assure that an instructor's typical teaching has been sampled (Braskamp 1978; Centra 1975). In practice, the number of visits has ranged from two per semester (Bell, Dobson, and Gram 1977; Sweeney and Grasha 1979) to weekly (Katz and Henry 1988) to every class meeting (Elbow 1980; Rorschach and Whitney 1986; Shatzky and Silberman 1986).

In practice, nearly all successful collaborative relationships have continued over a period of at least a semester. Katz and Henry, however, suggest that:

It is desirable for the two colleagues to work together for at least two semesters because the effect is cumulative, and frequently it snowballs. In our experience a third semester of work has proved especially beneficial because, with the interval of a summer, thoughts and attitudes consolidate. In our experience, when we walked into the class of a colleague with whom we had worked for two previous semesters, we were struck by the feeling of good will and enthusiasm that the new group of students exuded, a consequence of the different approach that the professor had developed during the past year's work (1988, pp. 15-16).

Limitations and criticism
Despite general support for formative peer observation, detractors contend that there are limits to what can be observed and that there are several potential threats to its reliability and validity. Wood (1977, 1978) describes ways in which the process can be biased:

1. Association (faculty who have close professional and/or personal associations are more likely to rate each other higher than those with whom they are associated less frequently);
2. Visibility (faculty whose offices are located near the central office are more likely to be rated higher than those whose offices are located in more remote areas);
3. Lack of independence between ratings for teaching and research (faculty who are rated high on research also are likely to be rated high on teaching);
4. Lack of independence between ratings for teaching and service (teachers who are rated high on service also are likely to be rated high on teaching);
5. Lack of independence between ratings for teaching and the number of credit hours taught (faculty who teach heavier class loads are more likely to be rated higher than those who teach lighter loads);
6. Lack of independence between ratings for teaching and number of graduate courses taught (faculty who teach larger numbers of graduate courses are more likely to be

rated higher than those who teach fewer graduate courses);

7. Faculty who teach elective courses are more likely to be rated higher than those who teach required courses; and

8. Lack of independence between academic rank and ratings for teaching (faculty who are at the higher professorial ranks are likely to be rated higher on teaching than those at lower ranks).

Centra has identified other potential threats to the reliability and validity of peer observation, noting that it has low inter-rater reliability, that faculty are more generous in their ratings than students, and that attaining a large-enough sample of classroom behaviors in order to make accurate generalizations may be prohibitively time-consuming (1975). While concluding that these problems are difficult though not insurmountable, Centra cautions that these factors should be carefully considered before peer observation is put into place.

Most of the concerns and criticisms of Bergman (1979, 1980), Centra (1975), and Wood (1977, 1978) regarding the reliability and validity of peer observation are made with respect to summative evaluation. Nevertheless, some of their concerns also are applicable to formative evaluation. While some have said such concerns are less important in formative evaluation than in summative, we would argue that regardless of the purpose, evaluators must strive to provide information that is accurate, fair (free of prejudice and/or ulterior motive), and, if possible, helpful to faculty in improving their teaching. But because faculty are not in complete agreement about "effective teaching," assessment may appear inaccurate, biased, or too subjective to faculty.

Because of honest differences of opinion on some tough epistemological issues, not because evaluators are incompetent, biased, or mean-spirited, reliability coefficients may be lower than hoped. As a reviewer of this report succinctly put it, "The bulwark of successful [formative] peer evaluation is an underlying commitment to building a culture of teaching, a collegial, mutually supportive, exploratory community interested in the teaching/learning dynamic," one prizing candid, free, and honest discussion and debate of epistemological issues affecting teaching, learning, and assessment.

Direct classroom observation has been fashioned in a variety of ways at colleges and universities where it has been employed, but it is not the only method of peer evaluation that has been used. These other methods include class video-taping, course-material evaluating, and assessing instructor evaluations of the academic work of students.

Videotaping of Classes

Compared with the volume of literature on classroom obser-vation, relatively little attention has been paid to how video-taping can contribute to instructional improvement. Never-theless, its advocates tell us what can be accomplished by video playback/feedback, how to implement videotaping pro-grams, and how to deal with its potential dangers.

Objectives

To many students of faculty evaluation, videotaping of classes is seen as an alternative to classroom observation. In some respects, it is, since videotaping also can provide useful infor-mation about what is occurring in a classroom and suggest ways in which instruction might be improved.

Justifying the use of video playback/feedback in formative evaluation is more compelling, however, when it can be shown that it should be employed in addition to classroom observation. That argument is made persuasively by Perlberg:

> *The unique qualities of video playback, and in particular its authenticity and high reliability, make it a powerful mediator in its own right and an important "helper" to all other feedback sources. [When a teacher has difficulty accepting feedback from students, peers, administrators, or teaching consultants], video recordings, giving both audio and video feedback, could validate feedback from [these] other sources. When all sources of feedback correlate, the person is faced with "reality in its nakedness," which is dif-ficult to deny* (1983, pp. 656-57).

Lichty and Peterson also note that videotaping can provide information that is difficult to obtain using other methods:

> *Since the video tapes are a permanent record of the faculty member's teaching performance, this technique of peer eva-luation provides several added dimensions to the measuring of teaching effectiveness. First, the strong points of each teacher's technique can be visualized and disseminated both*

*to the department and interested outside observers. No
longer will good teaching techniques die after delivery.
Second, the weak points of each teacher's techniques may
be systematically reviewed and studied for future correc-
tion. Third, a teacher may compare past video tapes for
signs of improvement or decay in his or her classroom
manner* (1979, p. 5).

A number of scholars have commented more specifically on
what informed peers could look for as they view tapes of
classroom teaching. Dressel observes that it might be used
to illustrate "weaknesses in delivery, in expression, in emphasis, and in attention to students—all of which can be
improved" (1976, p. 351). Smith and others add that in addition to weaknesses in presentation, videotaping can provide
useful clues to student responses to what was presented
(1988).

Craig, Redfield, and Galluzzo envision an even greater role
for videotaping (1986). They recommend that it be used in
"stimulated recall interviews," self-reports in which a videotape of a class is played and stopped periodically for students
to report what they thought about and how they reacted to
specific incidents at strategic points during the class session.
The same thinkers suggest that peers are well-qualified to
assist a colleague in interpreting the information provided
by the stimulated recall interview. It should be emphasized,
though, that "interviews with students should be construed
as the teacher's inquiry into how learning comes about, rather
than assessments of the goodness or badness of the course
or the teacher. Interview questions should incorporate suggestions from the teacher, and the teacher should conduct
at least some of the interviews" (Menges 1991, p. 34).

Procedures
Five practical issues which almost certainly will affect the success of videotaping of classes in relation to teaching improvement need to be considered. These issues are: how to get
teachers to participate, how long a playback/feedback session
should last, how much time should elapse between taping
and playback/feedback, what type of participant training
should be provided, and how many tapings of a class will be
required to determine typical teaching.

Studies by Britt (1982) and Keig (1991) have shown that

faculty are much less inclined to take part in videotaping than in other methods of evaluation. Indeed, as Perlberg notes, for teaching consultants, "the major problem is how to motivate faculty to be involved in intense experiential teacher-training programs, including [videotaping], which are perceived as stressful experiences." Perlberg recommends that the initial appeal for participation should be made to particularly conscientious teachers who want to improve their teaching and perhaps also to those with a "natural curiosity to see themselves as others see them" (1983, p. 657).

Longer playback/feedback sessions seem to be more effective than shorter ones. Most effective of all are sessions lasting 40 minutes or longer. Sessions lasting 30 minutes or more are more effective in affecting change than those lasting 20 minutes or less (Perlberg 1983).

Perlberg recommends that a professor look at the videotape of his or her performance on two different occasions (1983). A partial viewing, according to Perlberg, should occur immediately following the taping and should be "aimed at reducing stress and anxiety through reinforcement of the positive content, and focusing on points for further contemplation" (p. 648). The second, more extensive and intensive, playback/feedback session "will thus be free of many of the stresses following the recording. Having a preliminary [playback] also provides the consultant and the [professor] with time for contemplation and perspective" (p. 648).

Perlberg insists that participants must be trained in how to transmit findings to colleagues. He states that "one cannot emphasize too strongly the importance of receiving the necessary consultancy skills for effective use of [video playback/feedback] in higher education" (p. 658).

The number of classes that should be videotaped is a question raised in the literature but not actually answered (1983). Too few tapings would surely limit the representativeness of the teaching sample and its accuracy. This issue is addressed more fully in the section on disincentives.

Model

McDaniel's three-stage model of formative evaluation of teaching includes a prominent role for video playback/feedback. Its three stages involve having faculty establish standards of effective teaching; evaluate videotapes of their teaching, with the help of a teaching consultant, against the teaching stan-

dards; and view tapes of successful teaching of other participants and "discuss how the episodes illustrate the teaching
behaviors they previously identified" (1987, p. 99).

Potential dangers and caveats

The self-confrontational nature of viewing tapes of and receiving feedback from one's teaching either can be helpful in
improving performance or a debilitating experience. The
manner in which a videotape is presented to a teacher may
determine how praise and/or constructive criticism are
received. Nearly all writers on videotaping comment on the
potential dangers of this self-confrontation (Brandenburg,
Braskamp, and Ory 1979; Braskamp 1978; Brock 1981; Craig,
Redfield, and Galluzzo 1986; Dressel, 1976; Fuller and Manning 1973; Perlberg 1983; Seldin 1984; Smith et al. 1988).
Brandenburg, Braskamp, and Ory express well the sentiments
of many writers when they say that findings from videotapes
are "especially personal and descriptive; viewing a videotape
with a colleague is preferable to only the instructor viewing
it because the colleague can share his/her insights, can provide support in this confrontational experience, and suggest
improvements and changes" (1979, p. 12).

However, the self-confrontational nature of video playback/
feedback is a salient strength as well as a potential danger.
Without it, little of value can be accomplished. Perlberg
explains how much of the potential benefit of videotaping
can be lost if self-confrontation is not judiciously exploited
by program participants and peer reviewer(s):

> *Knowing that [video playback/feedback] could be very
> stressful and at times even harmful, they choose the easy
> way out—using [videotaping] in a superficial way, which
> minimizes arousal and stress. The client tries to avoid dis-
> covery or admission of discrepancies. The consultant col-
> ludes in the defense in order to avoid arousing or panicking
> the client. The video is used mainly as a mirror for observing
> external cosmetic phenomena, or other trivial behavior,
> rather than for focusing on the basic issues at stake. Thus,
> the most powerful available technique for changing behav-
> ior is wasted* (1983, p. 658).

Yet, as Brinko admonishes:

> *Video feedback is not for everyone. In many instances it
> can be a useful tool; in other cases it can be a threatening*

and stressful experience, actually inhibiting performance or even increasing those behaviors which are desired to be extinguished. This same reasoning can be applied to all methods of feedback: the literature on individual differences makes clear that a wide range of perceptions and preferences exist among people in their reactions to feedback and in their learning styles. Thus, different modes of feedback will be more informative, meaningful, and relevant than other modes to different individuals (1993, p. 582).

While intrusive and, to some faculty, threatening, videotaping can be a powerful tool for effecting changes in teaching behaviors. Trusted colleagues, trained in consultative skills, can help each other use video playback/feedback, in conjunction with other methods of evaluation, to improve their teaching.

Direct classroom observation and videotaping of classes are appropriate for assessing what occurs when a teacher and his or her students interact. We turn now to three methods designed to critique pre-interactive and post-interactive teaching events.

Evaluation of Course Materials

Students of faculty evaluation generally agree that informed peers are ideally suited to assess colleagues' course materials. Menges, in fact, claims that "no one is better able than a colleague to make knowledgeable comments about the accuracy and currency of teacher materials" (1987, p. 86). But scholars also note that few colleges and universities have integrated this method into the evaluation process (Cohen and McKeachie 1980; Seldin 1984, 1993c; Weimer 1990). Moreover, a review of the literature reveals that considerably less attention has been paid to evaluation of course materials than to either classroom evaluation or videotaping of classes.

It is not altogether clear why evaluation of course materials has been neglected in practice, although some scholars speculate. Seldin, for example, suggests that its limited use may be merely one of oversight (1984). Centra offers three more substantive reasons: Course materials are so personal and subjective that faculty members are not willing to open the materials to the same close scrutiny that they give colleagues in review of manuscripts for publication; the time required to

While intrusive and, to some faculty, threatening, videotaping can be a powerful tool for effecting changes in teaching behaviors.

review course materials can be better spent on research where the extrinsic rewards are usually greater; and it is not worth the time because course materials are read "only" by students, while published research is there for everyone to read and evaluate (1986).

Nevertheless, one academic "is convinced that a great deal of unacknowledged brilliance resides in our colleagues' classroom strategies, in their syllabi, in their paper and examination topics, and in their paper grading—at all levels of instruction" (Miller 1990, p. 53). This assertion suggests that college teaching could be improved if peer review of course materials and assessment of instructor evaluation of students' academic work were a more common practice. At this point in the report, we look at what might be accomplished by peer review of course materials, what materials could be examined, how this method of evaluation might be implemented, and what the limitations of this method are.

Objectives

McCarthey and Peterson not only explain, in broad terms, what might be accomplished by peer review of course materials but also suggest, somewhat more subtly, why assessment of course materials should be combined with other methods of peer evaluation if the full range of teachers' competencies is to be ascertained. They write:

> Teacher materials yield factual and objective data for peers to judge. These materials provide an overview of the curriculum taught, information about teaching strategies, and details about assignments given. Materials can indicate types of communication with students . . . and peers, the kind of management system used, and resources provided to students. Peer review of materials gives teachers the opportunity to demonstrate excellence through the content and activities of the classroom, and to reflect teacher individuality. Finally, there is a plausible logical connection between quality materials and quality classroom performance for many, but not all, teachers (1988, p. 261).

Process

Several scholars have identified competencies faculty should have in course planning, instructional design, and test preparation that could be assessed by peer review of course materials (Aleamoni 1981, 1984; Brandenburg, Braskamp, and Ory 1979; Braskamp 1978; Cancelli 1987; Centra 1986; Cohen and McKeachie 1980; Dienst 1981; Eckert 1950; McCarthey and Peterson 1988; Scriven 1980, 1983, 1985; Seldin 1984; Smith 1985; Smith et al. 1988; Weimer 1990). Figure 5 is a compilation of the work of these scholars. In the figure, the categories are organized by the medium from which information could be obtained. In some instances, these competencies could be placed under more than one heading. In other instances, the competencies may be appropriate for some academic disciplines but not for others.

FIGURE 5

Guide to Evaluation of Course Materials

Syllabus
Instructor demonstrates command of course content
The breadth and depth of course content are appropriate
Emphasis and time given to each major topic is appropriate
The course content is an adequate prerequisite to other courses
Course objectives are specific enough to constitute a really useful
    guide in selecting and organizing class activities
Content is organized logically, in a way that seems meaningful to
    students at this level of preparation
The sequence of topics to be covered is appropriate
Difficulty level of the course is appropriate for its curricular level
    and for the students enrolled
Goals and objectives are stated clearly
Course goals and objectives are in line with department and/or college goals and objectives
Syllabus helps orient students to their learning tasks
Method(s) of instruction is/are suitable for course goals and
    objectives
Student work requirements for the course are appropriate
Standards used for grading are communicated clearly to students
Syllabus is revised periodically to reflect recent scholarship, changing
    student needs, more sophisticated thinking about the teaching
    of the course, etc.
Content duplicates/does not duplicate that of other course(s)

Readings and Other Learning Activities
The work of recognized authorities in the field is included in
    readings

Basic concepts of the content area are covered in readings and/or other learning activities

Readings reflect discriminating choice of books and/or journal articles

Content is up-to-date; instructional materials include recent developments in content

Readings are appropriate for the level of the course

Reading assignments require an appropriate amount of time and effort to complete

Course materials challenge and stimulate students intellectually

Handouts and other learning aids are suitable adjuncts to primary instructional materials

Media materials (e.g., films, videotapes, audiotapes, multimedia, computer programs) are used in appropriate ways

Community resources are used appropriately to supplement class presentations and other learning activities

Tests, Papers, Projects, Presentations, and Other Assigned Academic Work

Test content is representative of the content of the unit under study (test exhibits content validity)

Test items are clear and well-written

Tests require appropriate lower-level and higher-level cognitive skills

Criteria for the grading of tests (and other assignments) are appropriate and clearly communicated to students

Tests are reasonable in length and difficulty

Assigned academic work is appropriate to course level

Students apply principles learned from class presentations and readings in papers, projects, presentations, and other assigned academic work and on tests

Assigned academic work can be tailored to meet individual student needs and interests

Assigned academic work requires reasonable time and effort to complete

In virtually all of his writings on faculty evaluation, Scriven emphasizes the need for teachers to be assessed on their knowledge of course content. He says, for example, that:

> *There must be careful examination of the quality and professionality of content and process; the three qualities here are currency, correctness, and comprehensiveness. Ratings must be made on the basis of a sample of 1) the materials provided, 2) the texts required and recommended, 3) the exams, 4) the term paper topics, 5) the student performances on the preceding, 6) the instructor's performance in*

grading student work, 7) the instructor's performance in
justifying the grade and providing other helpful feedback
(Scriven 1980, p. 13).

While not a strong advocate of peer evaluation in general,
Scriven concedes that evaluation of course materials "is the
one place where peer evaluation of a limited kind is appropriate" (1980, p. 13). At least some of the content knowledge
listed above is surely among that informed peers could assess.

Procedures

Smith and others recommend that the procedure for assessing
course materials be similar to that described for direct classroom observation (1988). They suggest having a panel of colleagues: independently evaluate a range of the teacher's
course materials (syllabus, textbook(s), reading list, tests,
etc.), based on predetermined criteria (e.g., currency, rele-
vancy, accreditation standards); meet to discuss their findings
and, if necessary, to arrive at some degree of consensus; meet
with the course instructor to discuss the findings, clarify information, and provide feedback; and write a summary report
of findings and recommendations. After the process is completed, the course instructor is asked to consider the findings
and then either plan for and implement changes or explain
his or her decision not to do so.

Limitations

There are limitations, however, to what can be learned from
evaluation of course materials, particularly when such review
is conducted independently of other methods of evaluation.
McCarthey and Peterson note that:

> *Even when peer evaluation does not involve classroom visits,*
> *but is restricted to a review of materials, there are signif-*
> *icant reservations. Not all teachers are effective through their*
> *materials; some excellent teachers work with spartan pro-*
> *visions. The time cost of materials assembly may not be jus-*
> *tified by the increase in information provided. Some*
> *teachers seriously object to peer review, while the connection*
> *between peer review and teacher quality is not always*
> *direct. Peer review is intermediate in expense relative to*
> *other data sources; student surveys, for example, cost less*
> *money and time. Mere collections of good materials have*

*little direct relation to quality implementation, interactions
with students, and creativity in presentation* (1988, p. 261).

Faculty colleagues are in a better position than students,
administrators, and teaching consultants to evaluate course
materials. Informed peers can help colleagues look at these
materials in context of objectives, presentation, and outcomes.
Peer evaluation of such materials, used in conjunction with
other methods of evaluation, including the one we look at
next, has the potential to improve teaching and student
learning.

Assessment of Instructor Evaluations of the Academic Work of Students

Assessment of instructor evaluations of the academic work
of students is, in one sense, a dimension of evaluation of
course materials. In another sense, it is considerably different
because its focus is on a kind of teacher performance occurring, in large part, following delivery of instruction rather than
in course planning or at times when students and a teacher
are interacting. Since the two methods of evaluation may have
different impacts on students, evaluation of instructor-graded
student assignments is treated in its own right here.

Like evaluation of course materials, assessment of instructor
evaluations of students' academic work has only occasionally
been employed in higher education (Seldin 1984, 1993c).
And even where these methods are addressed in the literature,
disentangling information about them often is difficult. That
problem notwithstanding, we look at what might be accomplished by assessment of instructor evaluations of the academic
work of students, at what might be examined, at how it could
be implemented, and at some of its limitations.

Objectives
Thoughtful comments concerning an instructor's responsibilities in facilitating student learning, in a sense a rationale
for including peer review of instructor-graded student assignments as part of the process of evaluation, have been articulated by Dressel.

> *[It is an instructor's responsibility] to provide the student
> with satisfaction through a sense of progress. The respon-
> sibility requires pointing out to the student both successes*

and deficiencies. . . . Evaluation for feedback and moti-
vation is an essential component of good teaching. [Little
can] replace the personal commendation of an admired
teacher. Praise or the regard of others is a potent motivator.

[Yet] an indispensable aspect of learning is the recognition
and admission of error, combined with the ability to profit
from error. Failure must come to be regarded as a chal-
lenge, not as a disabling or uncorrectable event which
impedes further progress (1976, p. 343).

Dressel implies that a teacher's feedback to students requires
a balance between praise and constructive criticism, a point
not easily achieved. The academic work of students includes
an array of activities depending on their fields of study: tests,
papers, book reviews, projects, presentations, performances,
laboratory and studio work, field work, and homework. All
of these present opportunities for teachers to give relevant
information to students about their academic performance,
opportunities that are not always used to full advantage.
McKeachie, for example, observes that teachers too rarely
exploit the potential of tests in providing meaningful feedback
to students and suggests that if faculty colleagues were to
review graded tests (and other assignments), they could assist
each other in providing accurate and appropriate feedback
to students (1986).

Bryant also provides grist for peer review of instructor evaluations of students' academic work:

The real proof of a teacher's competence is how much his
students learn and what the teacher expects of them. Accord-
ingly, the examinations given by a professor should be scru-
tinized . . . and his students' papers should be read [by col-
leagues] carefully. If a professor obtains a high level of
performance from his students, he may be an effective
teacher, whether his students consider him a good buddy
or not. Admittedly, . . . evaluations would have to be made
with intelligence, but one hopes there is still some of that
quality available in our universities (1967, p. 329).

Feedback need not be confined to written comments. A conference in which an instructor candidly and tactfully discusses
the strengths and weaknesses of an assignment with a student

is another. Still another means is through audiotape, as Katz and Henry describe:

> One professor . . . began his course with the practice, continued throughout the semester, of dictating his responses to the written work of his students on a tape. (Each student provided a tape for repeated dictations). This practice not only allowed for a more personal and relaxed communication—students commented favorably on the tape, which always started out "Dear Jim" or "Dear Jane"—but also eschewed the usually greater finality of written comments (1988, p. 16).

Faculty need to develop skills in giving feedback to students and to seize opportunities for offering it in appropriate ways.

Process
A number of scholars attempt to explain with some specificity what peer reviewers should look for when they read instructors' evaluations of the academic work of students (Braskamp 1978; Dienst 1981; Scriven 1980; Seldin 1984). A compilation of their suggestions as well as some of our own ideas are provided as Figure 6. (We are indebted to Scriven [1980] for items appearing under the first entry.)

In insisting that more attention be given to the way in which faculty prepare and grade tests, Scriven states:

> There are professionally required standards here, with which virtually no faculty member at universities have the slightest familiarity. As a remedy for this, administrators should request that as a normal part of the process of talking about self-improvement, the instructor fills out a form indicating how papers are in fact graded (1980, p. 15).

Faculty whose knowledge on these matters is deficient or limited should be referred to colleagues with expertise in tests and measurements.

Procedures
A procedure similar to the one proposed by Smith and others for peer evaluation of course materials could also be employed for assessment of instructor evaluations of students' academic work (1988). The procedure might involve having

FIGURE 6

Guide to Assessment of Instructor Evaluations of the Academic Work of Students

Tests
Tests are graded in a fair and consistent matter:
- "blind" (protecting the anonymity of students when papers are graded)
- question by question, rather than test by test (to avoid the "halo effect" resulting from having read a particularly good, or bad, first answer of a student just before reading another answer)
- the first few graded answers are read again after reading all answers (to see if grading standards have gone up or down)
- papers are shuffled after reading answers to each question (so that students fare equally in the teacher's initial optimism or fatigue as answers are read)

Responses indicate that students use higher-order, as well as lower-level, thinking
Teacher provides constructive feedback to students
Teacher uses a variety of means (oral as well as written) to provide feedback to students
Standards used for grading are communicated to and understood by students
Tests are graded and returned promptly to students

Papers, Projects, Presentations, and Other Academic Work
All assignments are evaluated in a fair and consistent manner
Academic work submitted by students for evaluation indicates that students employ higher-level, as well as lower-level, thinking
Teacher provides constructive feedback to students on all academic work submitted for evaluation
Teacher employs a variety of means—written and oral—in providing feedback to students
Standards used for evaluating different forms of academic work are clearly communicated to and understood by students
Assignments are graded and returned promptly to students
Assignments submitted by students are of acceptable (or better) quality

a panel of colleagues: independently evaluate a representative sample of students' course work, assessing the grading of the work and the quality of the feedback students received; meet to discuss the findings and to make tentative recommendations; meet with the course instructor to share and clarify information and to present findings and recommendations;

and write a summary report of the review. Following the meeting with the panel, the course instructor would be given an opportunity to respond to the report, agreeing to implement changes or explaining a decision not to do so.

Limitations

When colleagues are called upon to assess instructor evaluations of the academic work of students, they may be tempted to evaluate student learning rather than to critique the appropriateness of the grading of the student work and the instructor's feedback to students. Therein lies a potential problem.

Scholars warn that assessing student achievement on the basis of instructor-graded student assignments (or even standardized tests), be it by colleagues or administrators, involves difficult psychometric problems. In this regard, Centra concludes that "there is at this time no evidence that these assessments will be valid or reliable" (1986, p. 4). The same author notes that this kind of evaluation is especially problematical, because variables besides teaching affect student learning. In expanding on and clarifying that argument, Menges explains:

> *Some argue that changes in students constitute the information of greatest relevance for teaching improvements. Examinations, papers, lab reports, and other graded work are undoubtedly informative, as is information about students' study habits and their scores on standardized tests. The major problems with using information about learning to improve teaching are that graded work is an incomplete representation of intended learning outcomes, it is difficult to connect particular features of teaching with specific learning outcomes, and some important influences on learning are beyond the teacher's control* (1991, p. 30).

Cohen and McKeachie take a slightly different, though still cautious, view (1980). They conclude that "colleagues, who have a sense of typical student performance, are in the best position to judge the instructional impact on students. As of now, though, such judgments are qualitative in nature and can be best used for supplementing other data" (p. 151).

The temptation to place too much emphasis on student outcomes can be avoided in large part by limiting assessment of instructor evaluations of the academic work of students to how well teachers grade their students' work and to the quality of feedback students receive. Another way to reduce the likelihood that one aspect of the procedure will be over-emphasized is to employ a variety of methods and several data-providing constituencies in the formative evaluation process.

The potential of assessment of instructor evaluations of the academic work of students is, in many respects, an unexplored area in the formative evaluation of teaching. It is possible that it may have a more significant place in the future, especially if faculty are encouraged to develop teaching portfolios as part of a process to improve teaching.

Teaching Portfolios

Teaching portfolios are collections of materials assembled by faculty members to document what and how they teach and to explain why they teach as they do. Seldin suggests that a teaching portfolio is a means by which faculty "display their teaching accomplishments for examination by others. And, in the process, [portfolios] contribute both to solid personnel decisions and to the professional development of individual faculty members" (1991, p. 3).

When assembled for the purpose of formative evaluation, Edgerton, Hutchings, and Quinlan observe:

> *Portfolios invite faculty participation in the examination of* one another's *teaching [emphasis theirs]. Faculty can work collaboratively in constructing their portfolios, they can also use portfolios as windows to view and share per-spectives on one another's teaching. Such collaboration is almost certain to be powerful when the aim is* to improve teaching *[emphasis ours]* (1991, p. 3).

In compiling a portfolio, faculty usually include "artifacts of teaching" such as course syllabi, reading lists, tests, and the daily work, papers, and laboratory exercises of their students. They also may include "reproductions and representations of what happened"—videotapes, photographs, diaries, jour-nals, and the student evaluations of their courses (Edgerton, Hutchings, and Quinlan 1991, p. 7). The 1986 publication, *The Teaching Dossier*, of the Canadian Association of Univer-sity Teachers, lists 49 "possible items for inclusion" under the headings "The Products of Good Teaching," "Material from

Oneself," and "Information from Others."

Compiling the materials is only part of assembling a portfolio. An equally important part is the reflection on, or self-assessment of, the materials included. As they reflect on the materials included, faculty may comment on what worked well, what wasn't as successful, what might be tried as alternatives, and what might be modified or discarded. At this point in the process, the focus is on why and how, not on what.

The portfolio process has much to commend it—it can be comprehensive, can reflect individual uniquenesses, and can involve peers in discussion about this central aspect of their work. Of course, the use of portfolios is not without problems. Shulman captures this tension when he suggests that portfolios:

> *are messy to construct, cumbersome to store, difficult to score, and vulnerable to misrepresentation. But in ways that no other assessment method can, portfolios provide a connection to the contexts and personal histories that characterize real teaching and make it possible to document the unfolding of both teaching and learning over time* (1988, p. 36).

It is important not to gloss over the barriers that exist to the effective use of this technique. Initial acceptance of and commitment to this process by a faculty is a major potential obstacle. There is no doubt that it can be time-consuming for both the person assembling and those who are reviewing it. The criteria for evaluation can vary. And perhaps most troubling in that our primary concern is formative evaluation, it can be difficult to maintain the separation between formative (developmental—for teaching improvement) and summative (for personnel decisions) evaluation. Once a portfolio is assembled and assessed, the result of the process is at least in the collective mind of those peers involved; it also may become a historical artifact in a file, unless stipulated otherwise in the guidelines for the process.

At the same time, it should be noted that multiple examples of successful implementations exist. Anderson profiles 25 such examples in *Campus Use of the Teaching Portfolio* (1993). One example comes from Gordon College in Wenham, Mass., where a portfolio-like process has been used in the tenure and promotion decisions for a number of years. This has made the transition to a faculty-development portfolio process easier than in other places without such a history. Starting on a small scale in 1992 with four faculty, three-quarters of the faculty now voluntarily participate in a portfolio-development process.

The key element in the portfolio, in addition to syllabi and reflection on their work, is the piece on "lessons learned" at Gordon College. The compiled portfolio is reviewed by a faculty-development committee and the academic dean, who gives one-on-one qualitative feedback. Faculty participating report satisfaction, noting growth in this aspect of their professional lives. Gordon College's experience suggests that new efforts start on a small scale, with voluntary participation, and, ideally, involve well-respected teachers as mentors in the process.

The objective of peer review of teaching portfolios, peer evaluation of course materials, and peer assessment of instructor evaluations of the academic work of students is essentially the same: better teaching. The differences among them lie in how this objective is to be accomplished.

Our primary intent in discussing the teaching portfolio has been to draw parallels between it and the evaluation of course materials and the assessment of instructor evaluations of the academic work of students. We have not attempted to explain fully the potential and limitations of portfolios, since the topic has been treated extensively in several recent publications (e.g., Anderson 1993; Centra 1993; Edgerton, Hutchings, and Quinlan 1991; Hutchings 1993; Seldin 1991, 1993b; and others).

Important as classroom observation, video playback/feedback, evaluation of course materials, assessment of instructor evaluations of students' academic work, and analysis of teaching portfolios are in formative peer evaluation of teaching, they are but five available methods. Other methods that could be used are those in which the input of faculty and students are combined. These include course instructor and faculty colleague interviews of individual students and/or groups of students and stimulated recall interviews in which students describe and reflect on specific events that occurred during a class session.

The methods described in this section present viable opportunities for improving college teaching. While each of them

The compiled portfolio is reviewed by a faculty-development committee and the academic dean, who gives one-on-one qualitative feedback.

can be used by itself, a combination of these methods—a comprehensive approach—is more desirable if the full range of teacher competencies is to be critiqued. To have credibility with faculty, this comprehensiveness may be indispensable.

In the following section, we look at a number of program examples. While none of them is comprehensive, at least in the sense described in this report, we recommend that readers study all of them carefully, for each has worthy elements and each has enjoyed success at least on one college or university campus.

FORMATIVE PEER EVALUATION PROGRAM EXAMPLES

The methods of formative peer evaluation discussed thus far have been put into place at relatively few colleges and universities. Surprisingly, no fully comprehensive programs, as we envision them, have been identified. While some are broader in scope than others, most rely heavily, or even entirely, on one method, usually direct classroom observation. However, the push to have faculty develop teaching portfolios, and interest in instructional improvement in general, may indicate that more inclusive programs are in the offing.

In this section, we look first at single-institution formative peer evaluation programs. Since fully comprehensive programs have yet to be put in place, we organize our discussion of these programs around the method employed most prominently: direct classroom observation, videotaping of classes, and evaluation of course materials and of instructor assessment of students' academic work. Second, we describe two multi-institution programs. Third, we assess the strengths and weaknesses of the programs described. Fourth, we look at their common elements. Finally, we explain how formative peer review programs have traditionally been evaluated and suggest how this process might be improved.

Single-Institution Programs
Direct classroom observation
Formative peer observation programs have been described more often than other methods. Peer review of this type has been developed at California State University, Sacramento (Stoner and Martin 1993), Evergreen State College (Elbow 1980, 1986), New York University (Rorschach and Whitney 1986), Texas Tech University (Skoog 1980), University of Birmingham, England (Mathias and Rutherford 1982a, 1982b), University of Cincinnati (Sweeney 1976; Sweeney and Grasha 1979), University of Kentucky (Cowen, Davis, and Bird 1976), University of New York, Cortland (Statzky and Silberman 1986), University of New York, Stony Brook (Katz and Henry 1988), and University of South Carolina (Bell, Dobson, and Gram 1977).

University of New York, Stony Brook.* At the University of New York, Stony Brook (Katz and Henry 1988), two pro-

---

*We refer to this program as the University of New York, Stony Brook, program, but realize that Katz and Henry's study, funded by FIPSE and Ford Foundation grants, involved instructional improvement projects at 15 institutions.

fessors work together, one in the role of observed teacher and the other as the observer, for at least a semester or, if possible, for two or three consecutive semesters. Both of the professors regularly interview students about how and what they are learning, and the professors meet frequently to discuss what is occurring in the class and what they are learning from the student interviews. Both professors and the students complete the Omnibus Personality Inventory (OPI), the results of which are used to compare the professors' and students' preferred learning styles. At the end of each semester, both professors write reports in which they reflect on what they have learned about teaching and student learning. Instructor evaluations of students' academic work can also be used to provide information.

While flexible in many respects, the process also has prescribed elements. Ideally, as Katz and Henry point out:

The colleague visits the professor's class once a week (or more often if desirable and if time permits), meets with the professor once a week, and interviews three students individually. The interviews are designed to obtain as detailed a picture as possible of what and how students learn. These interviews provide the professor and his colleague with many data on the basis of which to chart what is happening in the classroom and what learning the students are doing (pp. 10-11).

The same six students are interviewed each week, three by the observed professor and three by the observer. One student in each professor's group should have a learning style (as indicated by the OPI) similar to that of the observed professor, a second student a markedly different learning style, and the third a learning style somewhere between the two extremes. As Katz and Henry explain:

The prime objective of these interviews is to gain as detailed a picture as is possible of student learning in the course under investigation. This includes exploration of student learning styles, the student's cognitive stage of development, and the student's interests, aspirations, personality, and social circumstances because all of these can cooperate with or defeat learning in the course (p. 12).

Another approach for eliciting information about course content and its presentation is what Craig, Redfield, and Galluzzo have called the stimulated recall interview. At Stony Brook, the stimulated recall interview is used in conjunction with classroom observation to:

> *inquire about the students' specific reactions to the class session preceding the interview, preferably a class the observer has watched. Specific parts of that class may come under special scrutiny and students may be asked to talk in detail about what went through their mind, what they thought and felt as a particularly salient event took place— the event being a teacher's presentation, other students' contributions, an interchange, a perception of their own* (1986, p. 13).

According to Katz and Henry, the program requires four or five hours of each professor's time per week. There are, however, ways in which the program can be streamlined, including making fewer classroom observations and conducting student interviews less regularly, but, as the authors observe, "there is less benefit if less time is spent" (p. 11).

University of Cincinnati. The program developed for the University of Cincinnati and other colleges and universities (Sweeney 1976; Sweeney and Grasha 1979) involves three collaborating faculty members, each having classes observed and each observing classes of the other team members. The program has five phases: goal setting, a first team meeting, classroom observation, subsequent team meetings, and program evaluation.

In the goal-setting phase, each teacher lists his or her instructional objectives for a class to be observed and indicates how the objectives are related to course goals. At the first meeting, team members discuss and clarify the objectives, determine the focus of each observation and the procedures by which data will be gathered and reported, and schedule the first round of observations.

When the classroom visitations occur, the observers compile relevant information in areas specified by the classroom teacher, using the methods and procedures that have been agreed upon at the first team meeting. The peer review may include methods besides classroom observation if the participants agree that other methods could provide useful information.

At meetings where classroom observations are discussed, "observers are asked to reconstruct the details of the session observed to establish a common ground of discussion" (Sweeney and Grasha 1979, p. 55). They point out positive aspects of their colleague's teaching and offer suggestions and possible alternatives in areas where they believe performance could be improved. The observed teacher is encouraged to respond to the feedback by asking questions, seeking clarification, and commenting on what occurred during the class. After the discussion, the observed teacher is asked to develop strategies to improve specific aspects of teaching, based on what he or she has learned from the observation process and from self-assessment. Finally, another classroom visit is scheduled.

After a team has completed a full round of visitations, the participants meet to assess the process. At this session, they attempt to identify their successes and failures and/or the particular interpersonal relationships which may have facilitated or hampered the process. Following this phase, the entire sequence of events is repeated.

Texas Tech University. In the true spirit of formative peer review, the program at Texas Tech University (Skoog 1980) "gives priority to data and suggestions that will enhance or build on existing patterns of strength in the faculty member's teaching repertoire" (p. 23). In practice, it is similar to the University of Cincinnati program, though it has distinctive features. The process is carried out by a team of players: the professor who will be observed, a colleague who serves as team leader, one to three additional faculty members, and, on occasion, a graduate student.

The process has five stages: pre-observation conference, observation, analysis and strategy session, post-observation conference, and post-conference analysis. At the pre-observation conference:

relationships are shaped, information is shared, and goals are set. . . . The observee tells the team about the session to be observed—its objectives, what instructional modes will be used, [and] what the student role will be (p. 23).

At this time, the observed professor and the team arrive at consensus on the aspects of teaching that will be assessed and the procedures that will be used to provide relevant data. The procedures may include videotaping and student interviews as well as observation.

During the observation stage, the team visits the professor's class, gathering the types of information agreed upon earlier. Normally, observers spend from 15 to 20 minutes in the classroom.

At the analysis and strategy session, where the observed professor is not present, team members attempt to reconstruct the events of the classroom visit. In determining its feedback strategy, the team compares information provided by the instructor at the pre-observation conference to what occurred during the classroom visit, trying to describe, not judge, the professor's teaching.

At the post-observation conference, the observed professor and the team of observers meet to discuss events that occurred at each stage of the process. As the team presents its findings, the observed professor "should be involved in asking questions and reacting to the team's observations and suggestions" (p. 24).

In post-conference analysis, the process itself is assessed. Of particular importance is evaluation of the effectiveness of the strategies employed during the post-observation conference, since that stage is vital to how the professor will use the process to improve his or her teaching.

University of Kentucky College of Medicine. The Department of Community Medicine of the University of Kentucky College of Medicine's peer review program (Cowen, Davis, and Bird 1976) is considerably different from most programs, because content of a proposed course first was presented to faculty observers rather than to students. There are two distinct components of the program. The first, discussed here, is limited to observation; the second, described later, includes peer review of course materials as well as observation.

The peer observation component has, in effect, four stages: a professor's presentation of proposed lectures to colleagues; general discussion about and written peer evaluations of the teaching; a professor's self-assessment, review of colleagues' written comments, and revision of the proposed lectures; and the professor's revised presentation to colleagues. In essence, course development becomes a more structured process, no longer left entirely to the course instructor's discretion.

University of South Carolina. The formative peer evaluation process at the University of South Carolina (Bell, Dobson, and Gram 1977) has not only elements in common with most programs—pre-observation, observation, post-observation—but also two somewhat different components. The program's sequence of activities are: an orientation session involving all program participants; a pre-observation conference between observed professor and observer; two classroom observations; post-observation conferences; and a debriefing session.

The orientation session includes a general discussion among participants on their expectations for the program, the identification "of teaching styles or characteristics that may distract from learning" (p. 16), the generation of suggestions for managing classroom discussion, and evaluation of "general communicability" of course content. The debriefing session, again involving all participants, is essentially program evaluation, but can also include discussion of issues raised in the orientation session.

Evergreen State College. The peer review program at Evergreen State College (Elbow 1980) is different in many respects from other programs. In some instances, the differences are fundamental; in others, the differences are in emphasis. One distinct difference is in the role played by the observer. At Evergreen, "one faculty member each quarter would be freed from teaching to be a '[designated] visitor' and would spend each week visiting a faculty member who had volunteered to be visited" (p. 25).

The process consists of a series of four events: pre-observation assessment, pre-observation interview, observation, and post-observation conference. Of pre-observation assessment, Elbow writes:

Well before the week of visitation, I asked the faculty members whom I was to [observe] to write informally about what they wanted to work on, the parts of their teaching that pleased or did not please them, the changes that they wanted to produce in students through their teaching, and, more personally, the satisfactions and dissatisfactions that came to them from teaching. I also invited stories about good and bad moments not only as teacher but also as student (p. 26).

The pre-observation interview between professor and observer is an opportunity for them to discuss what the faculty member had written for the pre-observation assessment and to lay groundwork for classroom visits. Elbow is precise in indicating what he hoped to accomplish at this point of the process:

First, I listened for statements of goals and problems so that I could see what I was being invited to do and the kind of permission that I was being given. I wanted to be saying, in effect, "You set the agenda for my visits and feedback. I will give you only the kind of feedback that you desire. You are the boss. . . .

The second thing I looked for in these initial conversations was memorabilia, anecdotes and portraits from the person's memory of teaching and of being a student. I wanted to hear about good moments and bad ones, interesting personalities who seemed important, incidents that somehow stuck in mind. This was a powerful way for people to find out more about their real goals, not just their professional goals. People often wandered into insights as they told me incidents that somehow stayed in their minds through the years (p. 27).

Over the course of a week of visitations, the observer is present at virtually all occasions when the professor and students interact. The occasions include classes, seminars, and individual conferences, even sessions in which faculty interact with others in the absence of students.

Prior to the post-observation conference, Elbow observes:

Before the final, long conversation at the end of the week (or the beginning of the next), where I brought together my most important perceptions and made my recommendations, if I had any, I usually sat down a couple of times to play back my perceptions of what had happened in a seminar, class, or conference.

I took extensive notes during the initial conversation and subsequent observations. At first, I wanted only to aid my memory—and perhaps also to cover my nervousness—but it turned out to make the process one of mirroring what happened—both in the room and in me—not one of reaching conclusions. Also, I found that I had more to say than if I sat back to observe and wait for wise insights. When I left the note-taking machine on full throttle, perceptions, reactions, nuances of feeling, and even metaphors readily came to mind (p. 27).

Videotape or audiotape recordings and interviews of students can be used to supplement the essential program components. It is information gathered in a number of ways that is the basis for the post-observation conference.

University of New York, Cortland. In the master-student scheme devised by Shatzky and Silberman at the University of New York, Cortland, two faculty members—from different academic disciplines—collaborate to improve each other's teaching (1986). Their aims are "to acquaint each other with an introductory course in a subject in which neither of us had any preparation," "to observe one another's teaching techniques from the student's point of view," and "to see what problems students have in comprehending the material discussed in each class" (p. 119).

In the role of student, the professor attends each class, completes all written assignments and projects, and takes all tests. The professor also attempts to converse informally with students about their understanding of course content and the professor's teaching.

A professor as student can be helpful to a colleague, according to Shatzky and Silberman,

in pointing out problems in presentation, the design of assignments, or even the line of questions on an examination. Skill and experience enable the colleague to diagnose and articulate such problems clearly and objectively. Provided the instructors trust and respect each other's judgment, criticism can be presented constructively—without the inherent ambiguities associated with student evaluations or the questionable value of one-time peer visitation and evaluation (p. 119).

New York University. In an attempt to learn more about the nature of teaching and learning and to improve their students'—and their own—performance, two composition instructors (Rorschach and Whitney 1986) describe a formative peer evaluation program they developed at New York University. They explain the participant-observer method as follows:

> *For 15 weeks, we attended each other's freshman writing course, which met twice a week for a total of three hours. . . . The teacher in each class taught as she normally would, while the observer took the role of a student, participating in class discussions, writing drafts for most of the assignments, and sharing his writing in peer groups with the other students. We each kept a notebook on the experience, and we met once a week for about an hour to discuss what had been happening (p. 160).*

Later in the term, when observation alone failed to provide enough information about differences in student attitudes and behaviors to satisfy the instructors, they also report using two additional data-gathering methods. They explain that tape recording of classes was chosen "so that we could look more closely at our classroom behavior. Though we shared a sense that we were behaving differently in our roles as teacher, it was not immediately apparent how" (p. 163). And they report examining each other's lesson plans "to see if any differences in the progression of each course would help us explain the experienced differences in the [class culture] we had produced" (p. 163).

Rorschach and Whitney also report discovering how to develop a classroom culture in which students share authority with the teacher and how students can be helped to develop a sense of autonomy as writers. The authors also are convinced that their participant-observer method has implications for changing the nature of the teaching and learning process for both students and teachers. They write:

> *The situation that we found ourselves in is not uncommon. Most teachers experience a yawning gap between the abstractions about education presented to them by university researchers and the pressing decisions about what to do in their classrooms tomorrow morning. Perhaps the fault*

Tape recording of classes was chosen "so that we could look more closely at our classroom behavior."

*for this gap lies neither with the researchers nor with the
teachers, but with the situation: the isolation of the one-
teacher classroom, rigid scheduling patterns, limited or nonexistent opportunities for ongoing collaborative inquiry, and
the lack of sufficient precedent and support for carrying
out such inquiry even when the opportunities for it could
be made. The great bulk of useful human knowledge, after
all, is probably generated outside of laboratories and librar-
ies by groups of people working to solve common problems,
talking and thinking together as they go. Through such collaborative inquiry we teachers can become researchers in
our classrooms and turn our valuable classroom experience
into useful knowledge for ourselves and for one another*
(pp. 171-72).

University of Birmingham. The "course evaluation
scheme" at the University of Birmingham, England (Mathias
and Rutherford 1982a, 1982b), involves the gathering of data
from both peers and students, and from a variety of methods,
of which observation is but one. According to Mathias and
Rutherford, the purpose of the program is "to help [faculty]
to find out how their courses were being received by students,
to identify areas of difficulty and to explore whether students
understand and could work for the aims [faculty] had in
mind" (1982b, p. 48).
The essential elements in the process are as follows:

*A common sequence of events would involve the evaluator
in the observation of a fairly self-contained 'episode' of the
course, usually centered around a particular topic. For
example, the evaluator would attend several lectures, tutor-
ials, practical classes or seminars as an observer. He would
then discuss the course with one or more small groups of
students employing a semi-structured interview technique
with the assurance that their anonymity would be preserved.
The evaluator and lecturer would then develop a questionnaire to follow up some of the main issues which had
emerged, as well as probing other aspects of the course which
had not been previously investigated. . . . This questionnaire
was administered on a voluntary basis to all the students
taking the course and analysed and interpreted by the evaluator and lecturer. A final report was prepared by the lecturer in conjunction with the evaluator. This report, which*

described the procedures and outcomes of the evaluation,
was presented by the lecturer for discussion at one of the
regular course evaluation meetings (1982b, p. 49).

Evaluators come from fields of study related to that of the
observed faculty member, though not exactly the same or
clearly unrelated fields. Evaluators are not selected from totally
different disciplines because "experience showed that it was
important for the evaluator to possess some familiarity with
the subject matter of the course if he was to appreciate the
course activities and the problems that arose from them"
(1982a, p. 264). But evaluators are not selected from the same
discipline either, "to avoid the potential embarrassment of
exposing difficult problems to a close colleague" (1982b,
p. 49).

California State University, Sacramento. In the Professors' Peer Coaching Program of Cal State, Sacramento, the peer
coach's primary responsibility is to facilitate his or her colleague's self-assessment of, and self-reflection on, teaching.
That role is not to evaluate, direct, prescribe, or even suggest
changes. Rather, it is to document what is taking place in class
and to conjoin the teacher in conversation comparing what
is actually occurring to what the teacher believes or hopes
is happening.

In effect, the coach is a mediator between the realities of
the teaching events and the teacher's perceptions of these
same events. Through these conversations, teachers reportedly
change "with greater purposeful innovation in teaching than
evaluation provided by others" (Stoner and Martin 1993,
p. 7).

In this intensive, yearlong program, voluntary participants
(requiring faculty to participate is expressly proscribed),

attend 14 two-hour workshops (seven each semester) to
develop specific coaching skills, and talk with other partic-
ipants about coaching and teaching. . . . During weeks
between seminars, participants spend time coaching. A
"coaching cycle" is completed when a participant has been
coached in a pre-teaching conference, observed by the
coach, and coached in a post-observation conference and
has performed the same functions for the partner
(pp. 8-9).

When participants meet in pre-conference to talk about the forthcoming classroom visitation, the coach employs "specific communication skills in questioning, probing, paraphrasing, and decoding nonverbal messages to [elicit from the teacher] precise descriptions of the lesson to be taught" (pp. 9-10). During this session, the peer coach engages the teacher in a discussion of goals and objectives, anticipated teaching strategies, the means by which student learning will be ascertained, and the methods and procedures that will be employed to document what takes place during observation.

A critical stage of the program is post-observation coaching. In these sessions,

> *Using specific coaching skills, particularly questioning and paraphrasing, the coach will assist the teacher in recalling the teacher's personal assessment of the class, the teacher's behaviors and decisions, and the students' behaviors, and assist the teacher in making reasoned inferences about relationships between student achievement and the teacher's thinking and actions. It is here that the coach will supply, if asked, to the teacher the specific data collected by the coach* (p. 11).

Pre-observation and post-observation coaching protocols are provided by Stoner and Martin in their text as Figures 1 and 2, respectively.

In that the program's objective is to encourage the teacher to assess his or her teaching accurately by comparing, with a coach's assistance, reality with perception, the Professors' Peer Coaching Program is considerably different from more directive formative peer evaluation programs. And, in that it explicitly empowers teachers to make changes in their teaching, the program promotes regular self-assessment. This is in marked contrast to episodic evaluations by others.

Videotaping of classes

The use of videotaping of classes to improve teaching is not apparently very common in higher education. Only one program of formative peer review in which videotaping was the central element is described in recent literature on instructional development. Otherwise, videotaping has been employed as an adjunct to other methods of formative

gram has evolved during its short life from what its creator, Joseph Katz, envisioned to its present form. It now involves having faculty: "pair themselves off, preferably with someone from a different discipline" to observe each other's teaching; interview students about what and how they are learning; meet as a pair to discuss what is happening in the classes being observed and what students are saying in the interviews; meet as a group with other pairs to discuss common and unique experiences; and write reflective essays on what they have learned about teaching and learning from the classroom observations, student interviews, and collaboration with colleagues.

The process of peer classroom observation, student interviews, and collaboration takes place over the course of, ideally, two terms of instruction. During the first term, one member of each pair observes one of the other's classes, once a week if possible or at least biweekly. During the following term, these roles are reversed. Like the program manual indicates, "the success of the process is greatest if the observer becomes an accepted part of the class (essentially invisible). To achieve this invisibility, the observer should begin early in the semester, and the observer should attend regularly" (NJICTL 1991, p. 8). While attending classes,

> *the observer pays close attention to the process and dynamics of the group. The observer notes the effect on the students of the instructor's presentation, the manner and types of questions generated, interactions between students, group discussions, non-verbal communication—everything that happens during the class* (NJICTL 1991, p. 9).

In PIL, the student interview is indispensable, since a "wealth of information and insight" about teaching and student learning is obtained in this way. Each participant—teacher and observer—interviews three students on several occasions (usually three to five times) each semester, focusing initially on rather general topics but eventually on more substantive matters relative to student learning. Interviewers are encouraged to select students representing "a broad section of the class in age, gender, race, classroom demeanor, or academic performance" (NJICTL, 1991, p. 10) and to employ a flexible, semi-structured approach. (Recommended interview protocols are provided by NJICTL [1991, pp. 10-12] and by Woolwine [1988, p. 49].)

Faculty pairs meet frequently (every week or two) to discuss what has been taking place in the classes observed and what students are talking about in the interviews. The critical initial meeting of each pair should occur prior to observations and interviews, for it is during this occasion that "an immediate intimacy between the partners [can develop, and an attenuation of] tension that either might be feeling about the observation process [can occur]" (NJICTL 1991, p. 10).

About once per month, all pairs on campus meet to consider topics of common interest. These topics include what is happening in the classes being observed and in the student interviews, problems encountered, teaching theories, learning styles, critical thinking, recent research on pedagogical issues, and the like.

At the end of each term, both participants write essays where "the focus may range from thoughts about classroom observation, student interviews, and interaction with colleagues to any facet of her own teaching that these activities may have led the participant to examine" (NJICTL 1991, p. 14). Where faculty give permission, their essays, or excerpts from these pieces, could be distributed across campus, allowing ideas and insights about teaching and student learning to be shared with colleagues.

Program coordinators, participants, and evaluators tell us not only that PIL works but also *why* it works and *how* it improves teaching and student learning. Steve Golin, Katz's successor as state program director, explains why it has been successful:

> *It works because the program is* ongoing, *because it is* decentralized, *because it is* faculty owned, *and because the process itself is* transforming. . . . *Faculty who observe and are observed, who interview students, who meet with a partner, are engaged in an ongoing process. . . . Feedback from our students and our colleague is continuous. In response, we try some new things, and we get feedback on them. . . . The faculty pair is largely autonomous. It charts its own directions. . . . The pair shapes its own version of the process. . . . Very quickly, faculty claim ownership. . . . Faculty respond with real creativity and initiative to a program that they perceive is not only for them but by them. Collaborating with a peer is itself transforming. . . . For*

*many faculty, the student interviews are even more pow-
erful for our self-transformation* (Golin 1990, pp. 9-10).

How PIL helps professors improve their teaching and their
students' learning is at least as important as knowing why.
The value of the program is addressed later, in the section
on Personal and Institutional Benefits, under the headings
Improvement in Teaching and Improvement in Student
Learning.

From idea to prototype
As we complete the writing of this book, the American Association for Higher Education, in cooperation with Stanford
University, is initiating a multi-institution study titled "From
Idea to Prototype: The Peer Review of Teaching." Coordinated
by Lee Shulman, researchers at the 14 participating institutions
(all research and doctoral universities except one) are "conducting small-scale experiments in peer review exercises
intended to reveal the 'pedagogical thinking' behind various
aspects of teaching practice [and exploring] a variety of strategies in being colleagues to one another in teaching as they
are in research" (American Association for Higher Education
1993, p. 18).

Assessment of Program Strengths and Weaknesses
To this point, we have described, in a rather detached manner,
several programs of formative peer evaluation of teaching.
Chronicling the development of these programs is important,
we believe, because it demonstrates that increasingly sophisticated programs, ultimately more successful in affecting better
teaching, evolve—rather than appear full-fledged—and will,
no doubt, continue to develop.

Some formative evaluation programs, particularly those put
into place during the 1970s and early 1980s, clearly are pro-
totypes, quite limited in scope and scale. Others, especially
those implemented in recent years, are more fully developed,
more comprehensive in scope, and more ambitious in scale—
two even multi-institutional. Some of these programs, or elements of them, almost certainly will have greater and longer-
lasting impact on improving teaching and student learning
than others. We examine now differences among these programs, noting what we consider their salient strengths, greatest
weaknesses, and critical limitations. We focus much of our

*Most
programs
involve
collaboration
between two
professors,
one being
observed by
the other.*

attention on peer observation, since this is a common element among most of the programs, the only one that invites significant comparisons.

Most programs involve collaboration between two professors, one being observed by the other. In all colleges and universities where pairs work together except Evergreen, the roles are reversed at some point, so that classes of both participants are observed by the other. We consider this reciprocity a strength because it encourages intelligent professional people to learn from each other. Such an arrangement may benefit one participant more than the other if one teacher is more experienced or competent than the other, but a mentor-mentee relationship can be mutually beneficial as well.

At Evergreen, by contrast, one faculty member (the designated observer) visits classes of different colleagues each week. There is merit to this arrangement, too, since he or she can attend to this role for an extended period, developing a systematic process for observation over time. It is somewhat limiting in the sense that fewer faculty learn from each other's strengths and weaknesses.

Other programs involve two or more observers. At Cincinnati, three professors collaborate in the reciprocal arrangement described earlier. Its strength lies in having a teacher receive feedback on his or her teaching from two colleagues. A potential difficulty lies in scheduling visitations and conferences. At Texas Tech, a team of observers visits a colleague's classes. The team approach is attractive in obvious ways, but disadvantages exist as well. First, it is a "single player," rather than reciprocal, plan, limiting because only one team member's classes are critiqued. Second, scheduling can be unwieldy, since several faculty are involved.

Among the most controversial issues with which program developers must reckon is how to pair up the participants. In the programs we've described, teachers and observers have come from the same field of study (New York University and San Jose State), from related disciplines (University of Kentucky and University of Birmingham, England), and from unrelated disciplines (Cal State, Partners in Learning, and SUNY at Cortland and Stony Brook). We have suggested self-selection of collaborative units, a process that can be guided by participants' objectives and needs. We've made further observations about and recommendations regarding this issue in the section on Methods of Formative Evaluation, under the subhead Direct Classroom Observation.

The number of classroom visits has ranged from two per term (South Carolina and Cincinnati) to weekly or biweekly (at Cal State, Sacramento, and SUNY, Stony Brook, and in Partners in Learning) to every class meeting (Evergreen, New York University, and SUNY, Cortland). Clearly, two visits is inadequate for developing close facilitative relationships and for helping colleagues affect significant changes in their teaching. Obviously, more frequent visitations can be beneficial but require a greater time commitment from participants— essential, we believe, if the programs are to be valuable to faculty and students. We recommend that visits occur as often as feasible, but certainly no less often than every other week.

In all programs except Texas Tech's, observers attend a full period of a colleague's class. Since there are many aspects of teaching that can be critiqued by colleagues, we are convinced that peer reviewers should remain in a classroom for entire class periods. We also believe that to do otherwise would disrupt classroom dynamics unnecessarily, even more than visitation does by its very nature.

At SUNY, Stony Brook, and the University of Birmingham, England, and in Partners in Learning, faculty interview selected students on what and how they are learning and observe colleagues' classes. We believe the student interview can be a potent force in improving teaching and student learning, because it invites a more comprehensive review, promotes the bridging of faculty and student cultures, and fosters the creation (or reinforcement) of a campus ethos in which teaching and student learning are valued. If included in formative peer evaluation, interviews should be conducted regularly by both teacher and observer. Yet, we realize that the student interview, like videotaping of classes or other methods, may not work for everyone, since some faculty may feel so uncomfortable in certain situations that the result would be counterproductive. Generally, formative peer evaluation should be tailored to the individual needs of participants.

An observer usually sits unobtrusively during the classroom visitation. In New York University's program, however, he or she is participant-observer. This latter arrangement can work, we believe, if the observer is accepted as a regular class member. There is the danger, though, that he or she might be viewed as "star student," a situation in which the naturalness of the classroom environment would be disturbed. In most instances, we suggest that the peer reviewer be a silent observer, observing process and result and then purveying that information to the teacher.

The process by which feedback from observations is communicated to the teacher varies somewhat from program to program. As envisioned by Katz and Henry (SUNY, Stony Brook), it is relatively structured. In other programs, such as those as San Jose State and SUNY, Cortland, the process is quite informal. At Cal State, Sacramento, the observer's role is facilitative and nondirective. Generally, we believe that feedback should occur in a semistructured environment, guided by flexible protocols like those recommended by Stoner and Martin (1993) and Katz and Henry (1988, pp. 112-25).

Some programs include occasions where all program participants on a campus meet to discuss common problems and issues on teaching and learning. While requiring even more of participants' time, such meetings can be intellectually engaging and a source of motivation for faculty. We recommend scheduling an orientation meeting right before the term begins and two additional meetings during the semester. Such occasions might include presentations or discussions led by experts in teaching and learning, although extreme care must be exercised in selecting speakers to be sure that what they may have to say is relevant and worthwhile.

In all but three of the classroom observation programs we've described, other methods are "add-ons," not integral components. At SUNY, Stony Brook, and in Partners in Learning, the student interview is an integral element. And at Evergreen, an intensive pre-conference interview (between teacher and designated observer) is a vital element. It is in the lack of comprehensiveness that we find most programs wanting. None of the programs include evaluation of course materials or assessment of instructor evaluations of the academic work of students as any more than an adjunct to observation. We are convinced that these methods should become essential components of formative peer review process, examined either as separate entities or as part of teaching portfolio analysis. In either case, a systematic procedure for assessing these products should be developed.

Common Elements

The programs of peer observation examined in this section have a number of common elements. These elements are offered at this point to guide practice.

1. Programs should be built on the premise that "good teachers can become better" (Carroll and Tyson 1981); programs should not be considered remedial.
2. Faculty participation should be voluntary.
3. The observed teacher and the observer should be trusted and respected by each other.
4. Classroom visits should be reciprocal (a faculty member should be, in turn, observed and observer). (Only Evergreen has a designated faculty observer.)
5. Observations should occur by invitation only (there should be no surprise visits).
6. Participants should determine in advance what aspects of teaching are to be assessed.
7. Participants should also determine in advance what other procedures, if any, are to be employed in assessing performance.
8. The lines of communication between the observed faculty member and the observer should be open (feedback should be both candid and tactful).
9. A balance between praise and constructive criticism should guide the feedback process.
10. Results should be kept strictly confidential and apart from summative evaluation.

Many of these guidelines also could apply to the use of videotaping of classes, evaluation of course materials, assessment of instructor evaluations of the academic work of students, and analysis of teaching portfolios.

Evaluation of Programs

In all instances, authors of programs described in this section report that faculty members believed their teaching had improved as a result of feedback provided by colleagues. However, evaluation of programs appears to be limited to self-reports of participants; at least, no information is available suggesting that more rigorous evaluations were conducted.

In two empirical studies of faculty development programs, modest, though statistically significant, improvements in student evaluations of faculty and in student learning are suggested (Erickson and Erickson 1979; Hoyt and Howard 1978). Whether the results of these studies can be extrapolated to formative peer review is not known. It is clear, however, that systematic studies of colleague evaluation should be undertaken.

No method of formative peer review of teaching has been employed widely in higher education. In sections that follow, we look at factors which may detract from faculty members' willingness to participate, what might encourage them to do so, and how programs of instructional improvement of this type can be valuable to faculty, students, and colleges and universities.

DISINCENTIVES

On its face, it would seem that peer involvement in the improvement of teaching is a commendable idea. And it also would appear that the methods discussed in the previous section, used in combination, should be embraced for the betterment of the academy. We know, however, that use of these methods by peers for formative evaluation has been negligible. A number of reasons have been cited for the unwillingness of faculty members to implement and participate in this kind of activity. Some of the reasons are based upon practical considerations; others are derived from more philosophical concerns. This section examines four of the salient factors that we see as disincentives to faculty participation in formative evaluation of teaching: academic freedom issues; representativeness, accuracy, and typicality; subjectivity; and time, faculty values, and institutional incentives and rewards.

Academic Freedom

Several scholars have considered the issue of academic freedom relative to evaluation conducted by direct classroom observation (Cross 1986; Eckert 1950; Edgerton, Hutchings, and Quinlan 1991; Edwards 1974; Farmer 1976; Hart 1987; Mauksch 1980; Roper, Deal, and Dornbusch 1976; Pew 1992; Sweeney and Grasha 1979). While acknowledging that there is often the perception that direct classroom observation by peers, administrators, or anyone else violates a professor's academic freedom to teach, scholars have generally concluded that academic freedom is not compromised by classroom observation, because the right of faculty members to determine what is taught is not circumscribed by the process of observation. That argument is articulated well by Mauksch:

> *Under the mantle of academic freedom, teaching is a secluded activity while research, also concerned with deeply felt issues of academic freedom, is acknowledged as an accountable and challengeable activity, properly subject to scrutiny and checks. While challenging the methodology and techniques of the researcher does not threaten his or her right to pursue inquiry, the presence of a visitor in the classroom is felt as limiting the teacher's right to choose teaching content and teaching process. Although there may be some risk that those in power will wield inappropriate influence over either teaching or research, the mere presence of a colleague, in and of itself, is no threat to the freedom of teaching* (1980, p. 50).

This undoubtedly is a two-edged sword. On one side, the presence in the classroom of a peer can evoke a self-conscious reflection not only on the manner in which something is taught, but on the very content itself—an opportunity for improvement in itself. On the other side, this wide curricular latitude permitted faculty members, while usually considered a great strength of American higher education, also allows room for criticism from peers who may not share views or approaches.

Academic freedom to teach is a time-honored tradition among faculty, but it also is a self-interpreted, self-imposed, and largely self-regulated practice except as circumscribed by the courts (Poch 1993). Consequently, the distinction between legitimate concern over free intellectual expression and a nebulous fear or distrust of any intrusion can become blurred, contributing to the perpetuation of uncritical, cloistered attitudes that may undermine attempts at the improvement of teaching. These realities have led scholars to agree that gaining the support of faculty in a process of peer review involves overcoming the perceived threat to academic freedom to teach. We argue that, in that process, it also may require the deconstruction of individual and collective conceptions of academic freedom in order to lay bare premises based upon fear or self-interest rather than those that may contribute to a larger academic integrity.

As early as 1950, Eckert, while advocating the use of direct classroom observation involving colleagues as evaluators, warns that it should not be put into place "without making exceedingly careful advance preparations" (p. 67). This advanced planning includes eliciting faculty support so that classroom observation is not seen as an infringement on their academic freedom.

Representativeness, Accuracy, and Typicality
A second disincentive involves arguments that methods ordinarily used to evaluate teachers are not adequate for assessing the full range of their competencies. Complaints of this type usually are aired in connection with direct classroom observation, but some of them also could apply to videotaping of classes, evaluation of course materials, assessment of instructor evaluations of the academic work of students, and analysis of teaching portfolios, if these methods were used independently of, rather than in conjunction with, other methods. Five

common complaints are discussed at this point.

First, classroom visitation is not sufficient for assessing all faculty competencies (Braskamp 1978; McKeachie 1986; Stodolsky 1984). Obviously, observation should be used only for evaluating what occurs when a teacher and students interact, not for what occurs prior to and following delivery of instruction, processes that also are vital to successful teaching. Different methods are required for evaluating these other competencies. For that reason, scholars almost invariably agree that several methods of evaluation, used in combination, are necessary if the full range of teacher competencies is to be assessed (Aleamoni 1981; Arden 1989; Arreola 1984; Blackburn and Clark 1975; Bradenburg, Braskamp, and Ory 1979; Braskamp 1978; Dressel 1976; Greenwood and Ramagli 1980; McKeachie 1986; Romberg 1985; Sauter and Walker 1976; Schneider 1975; Scriven 1980, 1983, 1985; Seldin 1984; Smith et al. 1988; Soderberg 1986; Spaights and Bridges 1986; Stevens and Aleamoni 1985; Swanson and Sisson 1971).

In adamantly objecting to using direct classroom observation as the sole method for assessing teacher performance, Stodolsky insists that it is:

> *unlikely to be fair because any given observation will not be representative of the range of teaching behaviors used by a [teacher]. Evaluators are mistaken if they assume they are observing typical behaviors of [teachers] with the usual procedure* (1984, p. 17).

But she concedes that "one might use observation as one type of information in conjunction with other materials that could provide a more rounded assessment of a teacher" (p. 17).

Classroom observation is most valuable to teachers, Stodolsky believes, when it is used for instructional improvement:

> *In formative evaluation, direct observation may be very appropriate if too much is not made of any given observation. Direct observations can provide useful occasions for dialogues with supervisors and colleagues. Specific occasions are what teaching is all about, and may provide a very appropriate focus for discussing improvement. Discussions and suggestions that follow observation of a teacher may be even more helpful if it is recognized that he or she might*

teach differently in different situations. Rather than assuming that one knows a teacher well after a limited set of observations, one might rather acknowledge the incompleteness of that knowledge (p. 17).

Second, even where it is employed, critics object to the usual practice of sending an observer or two into a classroom on one or two occasions. Most researchers agree that such a procedure makes it virtually impossible to obtain an adequate sample of teacher behaviors from which to generalize about an instructor's teaching (Braskamp 1978; Centra 1975; McKeachie 1986; Prater 1983; Scriven 1980; Soderberg 1986). The procedure could be vastly improved, scholars say, by increasing the number of classroom visits and by visiting all, or most, of a teacher's classes, although these correctives would require substantially more time and a greater investment of other resources (Brandenburg, Braskamp, and Ory 1979; Braskamp 1978; Centra 1975; Stodolsky 1984).

Third is the argument that methods used for evaluating teaching fail to capture the essence and complexity of the teaching act. McKeachie, for example, observes that teaching "involves value judgments, and the means for achieving these values is complex. Research has revealed that many variables interact in determining faculty effectiveness" (1986, p. 266). Determining how these variables interact may prove difficult using methods ordinarily employed in faculty evaluation.

Fourth is a perception that evaluators are inclined to focus too heavily on skills associated with effective teaching (Bulcock [1984] calls them "observables"; Scriven [1987] refers to them as "secondary indicators"). In so doing, critics say, evaluators may neglect several more substantive concerns, such as the teacher's knowledge of subject matter and his or her ability to communicate it to students and to inspire student learning, epistemological issues, the relationships between the processes of teaching and learning and the prevailing institutional and student cultures, and classroom dynamics. Bulcock suggests that formative peer evaluation may be useful in examining a range of teaching behaviors in relation to the contexts in which teaching and learning occur.

Finally, scholars and researchers have tried to explain how observers (or cameras in classrooms) can affect an instructor's performance, making evaluation of "typical" teaching difficult

(Bergman 1980; Britt 1982; Gage 1961; Hart 1987; Sauter and Walker 1976; Scriven 1980; Stodolsky 1984; Ward, Clark, and Harrison 1981). Gage, for example, observes that many teachers feel so threatened by visitation that their "performance may depend more on [their] nerve than on [their] teaching skill" (1961, p. 19). Hart, elaborating on this same theme, concludes:

> *No outsider, no occasional visitor to the ongoing intellectual community of class, can hope to understand very fully the internal processes, the codes and interactions, of that community. No mere observer can fully understand the roles of participation in the class. And this is an important limitation, for the roles of participation control what happens in a class and how such happenings are perceived and responded to. Moreover, the very presence of the observer, however quiet and withdrawn, is an intervention that alters the situation, changes what is being observed. As one [pundit] argued, "To observe a class is actually to observe a class being observe" (1987, p. 16).*

Other teachers, as Ward, Clark, and Harrison have observed, seem to "get up" for performances in front of audiences including observers (1981). These researchers have found that the teachers attempted to involve students more actively in classes when the participants knew observers were present than when no one was aware they were there. Situations like this also militate against evaluation of "typical" teaching.

In a particularly cogent way, Scriven succinctly summarizes a number of complaints relative to the accuracy of direct classroom observation and introduces the issue of subjectivity, to which we turn next:

> *First, the visit itself alters the teaching, so that the visitor is not looking at a random sample. Second, the number of visits is too small to be an accurate sample from which to generalize, even if it were a random sample. Third, the visitor is not devoid of independent personal prejudices in favor of or against the teacher* (p. 10).

Subjectivity
Closely related to the representativeness, accuracy, and typicality issue is the third disincentive, subjectivity. Faculty

The teachers attempted to involve students more actively in classes when the participants knew observers were present than when no one was aware they were there.

members often charge that evaluation of teaching results in subjective, rather than objective, assessments of their performance, and several scholars have looked closely at this issue (Aleamoni 1984; Arden 1989; Bergman 1980; Centra 1986; Dressel 1976; Edwards 1974; Jones 1986; McIntyre 1978; Prater 1983; Wood 1977). Other researchers have studied personality factors that may affect the accuracy of the evaluations (Ballard, Reardron, and Nelson 1976; Bulcock 1984; Maslow and Zimmerman 1956; Murray 1975).

Bergman (1980), Centra (1975), and Jones (1986) have cited the research findings of sociologist Talcott Parsons (1954) to support their claims that evaluation too frequently is based on ascription rather than achievement, on affectivity rather than neutrality, on diffuseness rather than specificity, on particularism rather than universalism, and on collectivity rather than self. In assessing the effects of these dichotomies, Jones observes that the first factor in each pair represents a personal approach toward evaluation while the second represents a more bureaucratic approach (1986). Bergman suggests that evaluators too often employ the more personal, or subjective, of these approaches (1979, 1980).

The notion that faculty evaluation may not be objective is probably affected to an extent by differing epistemologies on what "good teaching" is and on the proper roles of teachers in the process of teaching and learning. Since there is a lack of agreement on these matters and probably never will be complete agreement (Bulcock 1984; Smith and Walvoord 1993), it may be necessary—even desirable—to exploit and capitalize on this subjectiveness. As Braskamp (1978) and Centra (1978) observe, there may be advantages in having colleagues look at peers' teaching from multiple perspectives, especially when the purpose is to improve performance.

While it is likely that on occasion, and obviously regrettable when, inappropriate criteria are used in assessing teaching, the issue of "appropriateness" seems somewhat less important in formative evaluation than in summative, since what is appropriate in one context may not be appropriate for another (Bulcock 1984; Stodolsky 1984). Still, the perception that evaluation might be based on subjective impressions lingers, and it may be a reason why faculty are reluctant to participate in various methods of formative evaluation.

Time, Faculty Values, and Institutional Incentives and Rewards

Finally, a major disincentive to faculty participation in formative peer review involves their academic values and beliefs. Two key features of this factor are the time required and the nature of their institution's reward and incentive structure. Scholars observe that faculty have complained that the time required to develop, implement, and take part in programs to improve instruction is excessive and of perceived dubious value. While this complaint undoubtedly reflects the sentiments of some faculty, it is at odds with a finding indicating the willingness of faculty in independent colleges and universities to participate in various methods of formative evaluation (Keig 1991). There is, then, interest among faculty in colleges and universities where teaching is regarded as the primary professional role for instructional improvement programs.

Few would argue that most faculty do not care about their teaching responsibilities. In fact, many would say, "I could be a much better teacher if only I had time" (Lowman 1984, p. 213). What is really reflected by this comment is that faculty generally feel overwhelmed by the variety of things expected of them—publishing, obtaining grants or contracts, teaching, committee service, supervising individual research projects of students, and so on. All of this suggests that the time concern actually is driven by the incentive and reward structure of the institution. Many colleges and universities continue to place a premium on research and publication with a concomitant devaluation of teaching, which in turn militates against faculty participation in programs of instructional improvement (Carnegie Foundation 1990b; Eble 1988; Fairweather 1993; Lindquist 1979; Mathis 1979). It might be expected that faculty would be more inclined to participate in instructional improvement programs if college and universities made a strong commitment to teaching through their incentive and reward structures.

In the final analysis, though, as Centra insists:

Unless faculty members are willing to leave the evaluation of teaching to students, who possess only a limited view, or to administrators, who often don't have the time or necessary background, then they must be willing to invest their time in efforts in peer evaluation of teaching (1986, p. 1).

As substantial deterrents as these factors can be to discouraging faculty involvement in peer review for improving teaching, a number of incentives to participate have also been noted in the literature. We turn to them in the next section.

INCENTIVES

While scholars and researchers have noted a number of factors that may detract from the use of peer evaluation of teaching, they also have offered several suggestions for enhancing the process. In this section of the report, we look at ways the process of formative evaluation might be improved and at how it might be made attractive enough to faculty that they would be willing to develop, implement, and participate in such programs.

The incentives that have been proposed by scholars and practitioners are of three general types: attitudinal and perceptual, methodological, and procedural. They acknowledge the need to change basic attitudes of the faculty. They also believe that improving the ways in which methods are employed will make the process more credible to faculty. And they believe there are ways of putting programs in place that will help to allay the apprehensions, fears, misperceptions, and skepticism of faculty with respect to evaluation in general and to formative peer evaluation in particular. An aim of such incentives is to increase potential participants' "comfort levels" with such programming, so that they will come to view it as a natural part of instructional evaluation.

Attitudes and Perceptions

At this point, we look again at what were called disincentives in the previous section, believing they could become opportunities if examined critically. We treat each issue briefly, focusing on attitudes and perceptions we believe will need to be changed if formative peer evaluation is to become a more commonplace professional activity.

Academic freedom

Having classes observed, videotapes of classes produced and analyzed, and course materials and instructor evaluations of students' academic work examined by colleagues—or administrators—often are perceived by faculty as threats to their academic freedom rather than as opportunities for professional growth and development. Somehow faculty must be convinced that peer review is as necessary for improving teaching as it is for providing feedback on manuscripts planned for publication (Edgerton 1988). It is beneficial, not intrusive, since colleagues have expertise about teaching and learning that is theirs alone. As Edgerton, Hutchings, and Quinlan explain:

On most campuses, student ratings are the "method of choice" for evaluating teaching. . . . But there's more to teaching than what's critiqued on student evaluation forms. What's missing in such evaluation are precisely those aspects of teaching faculty are uniquely qualified to observe and judge: . . . those things Lee Shulman has in mind when he refers to "the pedagogy of substance"—that require peer perspectives and review (1991, p. 5).

Formative peer evaluation of teaching is a means by which assessment can be approached in a largely nonjudgmental, nonthreatening way, like the comments trusted colleagues provide on manuscripts faculty plan to submit for publication. It may be that faculty are more willing to ask colleagues to review their research because colleagues are a step removed at that point from a summative accept-reject decision. Such is also the intent of formative peer evaluation, where development—not decision making—is the ultimate goal. Summative evaluation is, of course, another matter.

Subjectivity

Faculty often charge that evaluation of teaching is subjective. And they're right. They may not realize, though, that it is really not possible for assessment of teaching to be totally objective, because there is the inevitability that evaluators' values enter into the process. As Pittman and Slate observe:

A system of values acts as a reference point or standard against which the selected information is compared. The very nature of values dictates that there is no absolute standard, but that an individual or a group of people determines its composition. A corollary of this is that changing the evaluating personnel can alter the value emphases and evaluation standards. There is no way to avoid this situation completely; no matter what the form of the evaluation or the criteria on which it is based, a set of values resides at the core of the process. This means that in developing an evaluation system, special attention must be given to anticipating problems that could arise from the value bases represented, the interaction between the value bases and the specific evaluation procedures, and the possibility of a changing value base, as well as to minimizing these potential problems (1989, p. 41).

About all that can be hoped for, they say, is for the academic community to adopt general standards upon which to assess teachers' performance. The specificity of such criteria may vary from a single criterion (for example, the college's mission statement [Pittman & Slate 1989]) to several (Licata 1986). In formative peer evaluation, assessing teaching against flexible—as opposed to rigid—criteria might be viewed as an opportunity rather than a liability, since that flexibility will allow for teaching to be described from multiple perspectives, prompting, it is hoped, a professor's self-evaluation of his or her teaching and self-reflection on critical epistemological issues.

Time, faculty values, and institutional incentives and rewards

Faculty probably will find time for any professional activity if they are convinced it is valuable to themselves and/or if they are rewarded for it. Because faculty at many colleges and universities believe they are promoted and tenured more for their research than their teaching, they likely are to be more actively engaged in the former than in the latter. Even though studies show that faculty are more interested in teaching than in research (Carnegie 1986; Ladd 1979), "some teachers feel forced to give up the intrinsic satisfactions of teaching for the external rewards of research" (Cross 1988). So, too, probably with programs of instructional improvement. Ways must be found to make institutional incentives and rewards attractive enough to faculty that they will make time available for teaching and teaching improvement. The resolve of top-level administrators with respect to instructional improvement is crucial if higher education is to demonstrate its commitment to teaching (Fairweather 1993). Ladd's admonition should receive careful consideration by those who govern our colleges and universities:

> The "teaching vs. research" argument is hardly a new one. It has occupied the attention of faculty and administrators in the past and has inspired numerous experiments to redress perceived imbalances. My argument is nothing more than that these efforts have largely failed and that today the teaching profession is tyrannized by a research model. The intellectual health of both academics and academe will be improved if there are renewed and ultimately successful

efforts to give recognition to the training of students in what is primarily a teaching profession (1979, p. 6).

Methodology

The methodological issues, first raised in the section on disincentives, are examined again here with a view toward turning them into opportunities. We treat these issues briefly, since correctives have already been alluded to or stated explicitly.

Representativeness, accuracy, and typicality

Faculty complain, with good reason, that teaching cannot be accurately evaluated when classroom observation is the only method of assessment employed. With that in mind, scholars almost invariably recommend that several methods be used and knowledgeable constituencies be consulted so that all— or at least most—relevant teacher behaviors are sufficiently sampled. In that connection, Seldin emphasizes that:

> *Faculty evaluation is a complex process, and no single source of data is adequate. The combined appraisals of students, colleagues, administrators, and the professor's self-assessment are required for reasonably reliable and valid judgments* (1984, p. 155).

The methods and procedures employed can include direct classroom observation as long as the process also includes other methods. Formative peer evaluation also could include videotaping of classes, assessment of course materials and instructor evaluations of the academic work of students, portfolio analysis, review of student evaluations of courses and instructors, faculty interviews of students, and the like, all with an aim toward providing information to faculty about their teaching that is valid, reliable, credible, and helpful.

Faculty also complain, with cause, that classroom observation is unreliable when a single class is observed on one or two occasions. While it probably is not possible to say with certainty how many visits are required to improve reliability, the number should be enough to convince faculty that it constitutes a representative sample of teacher behaviors, across the spectrum of courses taught. If the sample is too small, the program will surely lack credibility.

In practice, relevant information might be obtained in three or four visits (Brandenburg, Braskamp, and Ory 1979). For instructional improvement purposes, Katz and Henry recommend regular peer visitations and subsequent feedback—preferably one visit per week over a period of one, two, or three semesters (1988). On occasion, faculty have attended every class meeting (Elbow 1980, 1986; Rorschach and Whitney 1986; Shatzky and Silberman 1986).

There is little doubt that the presence of observers changes the nature of the "typical" teaching-learning situation, particularly when classroom observation occurs infrequently. That situation could be improved if observation were to become more commonplace and routine. The same could be said of all other methods of evaluation.

It is probably essential that peer reviewers look at what is occurring in all, or most, of a faculty member's courses, because faculty employ different approaches from one course to another. As Shulman observes, there are relationships between a teacher's degree of understanding of subject matter and the teaching styles he or she employs, that "teaching behavior is bound up with comprehension and transformation of understanding" (1987, pp. 17-18). The formative peer evaluation program described by Elbow, in which a designated observer is present at virtually all occasions when a teacher and his or her students interact over the period of a week, could be used to identify a teacher's strengths and weaknesses in each course, presenting suggestions for improvement, if appropriate (1980, 1986).

There is probably a close connection between charges that evaluation fails to capture the complexities of the teaching act and that it usually is focused on teaching skills, narrowly defined, and too rarely on more substantive matters. It can be argued that faculty, who know what teaching is all about, should define the ways in which the essence, nuance, and substance of teaching are determined and find ways of using that information to help colleagues improve the quality of instruction. Edgerton, Hutchings, and Quinlan, for example, tell us that "classroom observation is a desirable practice; it's a form of peer review that can indeed address the most substantive, scholarly aspects of teaching" (1991, pp. 5-6). Videotaping, evaluation of course materials, and assessment of instructor evaluations of students' academic work are also viable methods of getting at what's really important. And these are only the peer review factors in the instructional-

As Shulman observes, there are relationships between a teacher's degree of understanding of subject matter and the teaching styles he or she employs.

improvement equation.

It also might be argued that faculty and administrators, by allowing student evaluation of courses and instructors to remain the only real source of information by which teaching is assessed, contribute to a system whereby evaluation is focused on perfunctory skills rather than on "a pedagogy of substance." If faculty want a credible system of evaluation—for improving teaching as well as for making sensible personnel decisions—they must take the lead in creating and supporting it (Centra 1986, 1993).

Procedures

Up to this point, we have looked at issues raised earlier in the report. Now we examine four procedural issues that have not as yet been addressed, at least directly. They are: involvement of the faculty in the planning of programs of instructional improvement, establishment of standards of effective teaching, training of faculty in methods of supervision, and faculty as interpreters and integrators of information.

Involvement of the faculty in the planning of programs of instructional improvement

Nearly all researchers agree that the development of successful programs of peer evaluation are dependent on the support of the faculty and of top-level administrators (Aleamoni 1987; Arreola 1987; Austin 1992a; Brock 1981; Freer and Dawson 1985; Heller 1989; Licata 1986; Razor 1979; Seldin 1984, 1990; Skoog 1980; Soderberg 1986). Without the support of the faculty, Skoog observes that the process is likely to be carried out perfunctorily, rather than with a genuine commitment to instructional improvement (1980).

The essence of the argument for eliciting the support of the faculty in the development and implementation of programs of instructional improvement is well-stated by Heller:

> *A decision to engage in peer supervision has to come from the peer group itself. The key is ownership; if teachers do not feel they own the project, then they will think somebody in the central office has a pet idea that is being forced on them* (1989, p. 13).

Evaluation often is seen as an adversarial relationship between those who are to be evaluated and those who will conduct it. Brock cautions that careful attention:

> be given to the design of the procedures, to the inclusion
> of teachers in the process of design of the procedures, and
> especially to clear and repeated communication with
> teachers about the procedures. . . . With the reduction of
> threat comes the increased likelihood that teachers will effec-
> tively use evaluation data to make decisions about change
> in their teaching practices (1981, pp. 235-36).

The recommendations of Brock and Heller have been incor-
porated into the program of formative evaluation described
by Freer and Dawson (1985). This program, in which a reduction of the adversarial relationship was a primary goal,
includes seven recommendations for developing and sustain-
ing the program:

1. The commitment of adequate funding;
2. The involvement of as many teachers as possible in the
   initial planning stages;
3. An attempt to arrive at consensus when program decisions
   are made, so that teachers "buy into" it;
4. Teacher involvement in training programs or courses in
   methods of supervision;
5. Collaboration among participants as the program is
   implemented;
6. Involvement of teachers in the monitoring and fine-tuning
   of the program; and
7. A separation of the functions of summative and formative
   evaluation.

Freer and Dawson indicate that the program was received with
more enthusiasm than the methods of evaluation that had
previously been employed (1985). They are convinced that
involving the faculty in the program planning was a key element in a program's success.

Establishment of standards of effective teaching
Virtually no scholar or researcher is audacious enough to
claim there are absolute standards of effective teaching upon
which to evaluate performance. On the contrary, most are
likely to acknowledge "that there is no single or best way to
teach and that what is good practice for one teacher may not

be so for another" (Elbow 1986, p. 197). Or at least they pay lip service to that notion. Regardless, the standards issue is complex, and it deserves careful treatment.

Some academicians say enough is known about teaching that this information should be used as criteria for evaluating teaching (Smith and Walvoord 1993). But others say or imply that faculty, through discourse and consensus, should arrive at standards by which teaching is to be evaluated (Angelo 1993; McDaniel 1987; Menges 1991; Seldin 1980; Weimer, Kerns, and Parrett 1988). And still others believe that, because too little is known about the interaction of factors that contribute to successful teaching, it is counterproductive, perhaps not even possible, to use generic standards, maintaining that successful teaching is context-bound and influenced by several complex factors (Abrami 1985; Bulcock 1985; Cancelli 1987; Gray 1991; Mathis 1974; Shulman 1988).

Those who assert that common standards should be adopted are likely to support the argument made by Smith and Walvoord:

> We have to either measure teaching or live with a system where it remains unrewarded. So we must gather a panel of the best people we have—faculty, administrators, experts in relevant fields—establish the fairest and most accurate criteria we have, and then go ahead. And we do have some criteria. . . . We have enough research on teaching excellence to begin articulating criteria for certification, and by starting we'll get more research (1993, p. 5).

On the other end of the spectrum are those who insist that it is inadvisable to set down uniform criteria for assessing teaching effectiveness. They believe that pursuing common standards on which all teachers are to be evaluated is misguided because teaching is content- and context-specific, dependent on the personalities, backgrounds, and abilities of both teachers and students and contingent on a number of environmental factors. They would probably insist, like Cancelli, that:

> A system designed to evaluate this process must be flexible. It must be sensitive to those variations in teaching that make it such an exciting and challenging activity. Reducing such a vibrant process to a checklist of behaviors performed

would reduce teaching to a mechanical act. It may be argued, therefore, that the use of a system that allows peers to use their analytic processes to scan, classify, sort, and resort, the complex and unique sets of data presented in each review is the only way to do justice to teaching (1987, p. 17).

Lying somewhere between these two extremes is the view that faculty should debate and ultimately agree on the standards by which their teaching will be assessed. They insist that "faculty members themselves will have to figure out whether and how [general principles of effective teaching] apply to their particular disciplines, courses, and students" (Angelo 1993, p. 3).

A number of scholars doubt there are enough general principles of effective teaching upon which to construct viable programs of faculty evaluation. For example, Abrami contends:

It is time to abandon the notion of a single model of effective instruction or the ideal teacher and begin to think in interaction terms. . . . The question should not be "What is the ideal college teacher?" but rather "What is the ideal college teacher for different contexts (i.e., courses, students, and settings) and different goals, objectives, or desired outcomes of instruction?" (1985, pp. 223-24)

The interaction to which Abrami has referred alludes to the difficulties involved in evaluating teaching. Adding detail to that idea, Menges and Mathis observe:

Effectiveness in teaching depends not on a single characteristic but on the appropriate fit among many variables. These variables include the purposes of the teaching-learning encounter, characteristics and preferences of teachers and learners, circumstances of the teaching-learning activities and of the larger environment in which those activities occur, and methods used for determining success of the teaching and of the learning. Effective teachers monitor and manage all of these variables, ensure their consistency and fashion them into a pleasing whole (1988, p. 10).

Coming at the same topic from a different perspective, namely course planning, Gray concludes that "the process for assessing the effectiveness of instruction should be flexible because the situations and contexts of teaching are extremely varied" (1991, p. 54). In course planning alone, as Gray indicates, the process includes "knowledge and skill of instructor and students, unique needs of the discipline, level of students and the instructor, instructor's experience, delivery mode, departmental guidelines and instructor control, environment and resources, incentive systems and student motivation, and perceived roles" (p. 54).

The situations and contexts to which references have been made are consistent with Shulman's "knowledge and learning" construct, which can provide a useful framework for looking at evaluation of teaching—formative peer evaluation in particular and other components of comprehensive faculty evaluation in general (1987). Common criteria may be appropriate for assessing one category (general pedagogical knowledge) of the knowledge base. Common criteria may be less appropriate for other bases (knowledge of learners and their characteristics; curricular knowledge; knowledge of educational contexts; and knowledge of educational ends, purposes, and values). Such criteria may be inappropriate for the remaining bases (knowledge of content and pedagogical content knowledge), depending on who assesses the performance and how the assessment is conducted. It seems likely that the interactive effects of teachers' knowledge in these areas is unique to each individual.

Centra is convinced that qualitative methods of evaluation are more promising than quantitative methods for examining teaching in detail. This method is consistent with the view that evaluation must be adaptable to a variety of teaching and learning styles. In summarizing his thesis, Centra observes:

A qualitative approach would involve descriptions of classroom instruction based on the perceptions of the observers. . . . Descriptions by several observers will more likely reflect possible personal biases and the resulting narrative could be much more useful [than] rating scales and numerical judgments (1986, pp. 3-4).

Faculty need to consider the ramifications of the standards issue carefully. If they are not willing to do so, it is unlikely that evaluation, for whatever purpose, will have long-term credibility.

Training of faculty in methods of supervision-evaluation and of communicating feedback

Besides claims that faculty would be more likely to participate in formative peer evaluation if they were to receive training in methods of supervision-evaluation and of communicating feedback, there may be additional benefits. The availability of training in these areas may be essential if instructional improvement programs involving peer assessment are to be successful.

Providing training in methods of supervision-evaluation has been recommended for many years (Brock 1981; Cancelli 1987; Centra 1975, 1986; Freer and Dawson 1985; Heller 1989; McIntyre 1986; Menges 1987, 1990; Mikula 1979; Root 1987; Seldin 1984; Sorcinelli 1984; Weimer, Kerns, and Parrett 1988). But except for Perlberg's useful guidelines for training faculty in consultative skills needed for providing feedback from videotape playback-feedback, information about such training has been largely limited to providing training in how to conduct classroom observations (1983).

Information about how to transmit evaluation feedback from classroom observation is found mostly in the literature in communications, counseling, psychology, and organizational behavior. Brinko's review of this literature is an excellent introduction into effective ways of communicating feedback elicited from observation and from other methods of formative peer evaluation (1993).

Another purported benefit of providing training in methods of supervision-evaluation is to improve interrater reliability (Cancelli 1987; Centra 1975; McIntyre 1986; Weimer, Kerns, and Parrett 1988). Such training would require, in effect, that agreement be reached on standards of effective teaching, limiting perhaps some of the flexibility called for by several scholars and researchers.

McIntyre has developed a program for training faculty to conduct classroom observation (1986). In this program, a number of faculty members visit the same classroom as a group, compare their findings after the visit, and then attempt to arrive at a consensus about the strengths and weaknesses of the quality of the instruction. McIntyre reports that this approach resulted in a considerable reduction in the variability of the assessment.

But scholars also note that training in methods of supervision will not eliminate all of the problems associated with improving interrater reliability. Centra has observed that effective training programs require more time than many faculty members are willing to invest (1986). Bergman concludes that "even with training, inappropriate criteria would still be quite influential in peer ratings—if only unconsciously" (1980, p. 10).

While suggesting that teaching consultants are a good source for providing training in supervision, Sorcinelli (1984) acknowledges that it could also be provided by experienced faculty. Agreeing, Brock suggests that whoever provides the training should have expertise in such areas as:

> *audio-visual technology, ethnography, group dynamics, instructional evaluation, attribution theory, gaming and simulation, computer-assisted instruction, personalized systems of instruction, and philosophies of education. However, the attributes of greatest consequence for the consultant's effectiveness may be a commitment to student learning; an abiding curiosity about the relationship between teacher, student, and subject matter; an empathic disposition; a knowledge of local resources; a tendency toward self-disclosure; and effective interpersonal communication skills* (1981, p. 239).

Still another possible benefit of providing training is to increase awareness. By becoming cognizant of the wide range of competencies required of effective teachers, faculty may become both more accurate observers of the teaching of colleagues and more insightful about their own abilities as teachers (Katz and Henry 1988; Mikula 1979).

Yet, few scholars have addressed the issue of exactly what training should be provided. However, Copeland and Jamgochian identify six general areas in which skills should be acquired: interpersonal communication skills, use of low-inference descriptive language, problem-definition skills, classroom observation techniques, data analysis techniques, and skills enabling effective feedback (1985, p. 17). Also, Menges advises that:

> *Some time should be invested in improving observation and feedback skills. Training should cover, among other areas, use of appropriate paper and pencil forms to organize observations, how to select information for feedback which*

is new *information for the person being observed, how to differentiate descriptive and judgmental comments while giving feedback, and how to deal with colleagues if the situation becomes stressful. Role playing is a helpful technique for this training, and role play sessions might be stimulated by videotapes of teachers who are not members of the group* (1987, pp. 90-91).

Because teaching and learning are complex processes, evaluation of teaching is also a complicated endeavor. Solid training in methods of supervision and communication appear to be promising means for improving the quality of both formative and summative evaluation and for increasing the likelihood faculty will avail themselves of instructional improvement programming.

Faculty as interpreters and integrators of information

The process of instructional improvement would probably be enhanced if faculty were to become interpreters and integrators of information provided by students, administrators, and self-assessment as well as by fellow faculty members. The information gathered from those sources should come from a variety of assessment methods. However, the faculty's role in evaluation should surely extend beyond this interpretive-integrative function.

Student evaluation of faculty teaching performance continues to be employed more often to evaluate instruction than any other method (Seldin 1984, 1993a, 1993c). Most scholars have acknowledged that students should be consulted in the process but have generally argued that students should not be the only source of information.

Many researchers have studied the relationship between student ratings and such variables as class size, expected course grade, time of day, required vs. elective course, the subject matter, and so on (see, for example, Arubayi [1987]). While there is some disagreement as to how these factors affect student ratings, researchers suggest that these factors be taken into account when personnel decisions are made and when instructional improvement plans are formulated (Cohen and McKeachie 1980; Craig, Redfield, and Galluzzo 1986; McKeachie 1986). Cohen and McKeachie suggest specifically that "student ratings should be evaluated by [faculty] peers who know the circumstances under which a particular course was taught" (p. 151). These researchers emphasize that student ratings cannot be taken at face value.

Faculty members themselves appear to be divided on the efficacy of faculty peer review of student ratings of courses and instructors. Britt (1982), for example, has found that only 36 percent of faculty were in favor of having their colleagues examine student ratings. Dienst (1981) has found even less support (33 percent), but peer review of student ratings out-distanced support for direct classroom observation and evaluation of course materials. The findings from these studies are difficult to interpret, however, since it was not made clear if respondents believed the review was for summative or formative purposes.

In a more recent study, faculty attitudes toward several aspects of formative evaluation are examined. Keig has found that more than 62 percent of respondents to a survey indicated their belief that instructional evaluation would be enhanced by faculty peer review of student evaluations (1991). But this relatively high favorable response is considerably less than that for direct classroom observation, evaluation of course materials, and assessment of instructor-graded student work. Support for faculty review of student evaluations of courses and instructors and for videotaping of classes is essentially the same.

Yet if faculty are to play a really significant role in the evaluation of colleagues' teaching, peer review must extend beyond interpretation of student ratings of courses and instructors. If faculty are not willing to evaluate aspects of teaching they are uniquely qualified to assess, there is a danger that "what is 'peer reviewed'" is not the process of teaching and its products (the learning that the teaching enabled), but [merely] the observations and ratings submitted by students and assorted others (Edgerton, Hutchings, and Quinlan 1991, p. 5).

Faculty are clearly qualified to assess colleagues' teaching at various points of the process. They can evaluate what occurs prior to and following delivery of instruction by examining course materials, instructor assessments of the academic work of students, and teaching portfolios. They can also look at what occurs when a teacher and his or her students interact from perspectives different from that of students, through both direct classroom observation and videotapes of classes. The formative peer review process must include more than an examination of student ratings of courses and instructors, important as that function is.

As programs of formative peer evaluation are being considered, efforts must be made to develop programs that are attractive enough to invite faculty participation. Accomplishing that aim involves addressing a number of faculty concerns: intrusiveness, comprehensiveness, objectiveness, and institutional rewards and incentives. Gaining faculty acceptance also includes involving them in program design and implementation, in determining the criteria on which their teaching will be assessed, in programs providing training in methods of supervision and communication, and in the analysis of information provided by students and administrators on faculty members' teaching.

If faculty can be convinced to participate in formative peer assessment programs, there are, it appears, benefits for them, their students, and their institutions. We discuss these benefits in the following section.

PERSONAL AND INSTITUTIONAL BENEFITS

Scholars suggest that a number of personal and institutional benefits might be realized from faculty participation in formative peer evaluation of teaching. Some of their claims are based on hunches, others on theory, and still others on qualitative and quantitative research studies. In this section of the report, we look at the evidence supporting and qualifying some of the purported benefits. We examine four areas: improvement in teaching; improvement in student learning; improvement in faculty morale and in the collegial climate of the institution; and improvement in the tenure success of junior faculty.

Improvement in Teaching

Formative evaluation of instruction has come about largely because its proponents have not been satisfied that summative evaluation actually facilitates better teaching. Formative evaluation involving faculty in the assessment of colleagues' teaching has been developed and implemented because practitioners believe that faculty are more qualified than students, administrators, and other constituencies to evaluate some aspects of instruction, although few contend that peers are the best source of information about all aspects of teaching.

Evaluation of such programs often has been limited to self-reports of participants and too rarely subjected to more rigorous study.

Some programs of formative peer evaluation have been put into place at colleges and universities where instructional development officials have encouraged its development, but other programs have been organized and developed by faculty who are committed to instructional improvement. Most faculty participating in these programs have expressed satisfaction with the results, believing their teaching improved because of assistance received from colleagues.

While there is no particular reason to doubt participants' positive assessment of these programs, researchers note that evaluation of such programs often has been limited to self-reports of participants and too rarely subjected to more rigorous study (Erickson and Erickson 1979; Hoyt and Howard 1978; Levinson-Rose and Menges 1981).

A few relatively small-scale empirical studies have been conducted of faculty development/instructional improvement programs (e.g., Erickson and Erickson 1979; Hoyt and Howard 1979), in which researchers attempted to determine if student ratings of instructors improved when faculty participated in the program. In these studies, students have rated the faculty member both at midterm and near the end of the semester, with the earlier rating used as a covariate in the statistical analysis. The results of these studies have shown statistically significant, though modest, differences between the experimental and control groups, with the former showing the most improvement between the two rating periods. Whether results from these studies can be extrapolated to formative peer evaluation is not clear. Whether improved student ratings of instructors actually represent improved teaching also is far from certain.

Levinson-Rose and Menges emphasize that much of the empirical research conducted with respect to faculty development programs is methodologically weak (1981). They and others recommend that future studies include larger samples of participants, examine the effects of participation over longer periods of time, and consider the effects of volunteerism—as opposed to random selection of participants—on results.

Austin's qualitative study on the effectiveness of Lilly Endowment Teaching Fellows Program projects is more ambitious in scope than the empirical studies (1992a, 1992b).*

From her evaluation of this particular genre of faculty peer evaluation, Austin notes how the faculty's teaching improved as a result of participation in these programs:

Fellows often develop a deeper interest in and commitment to being a good teacher and, through their exposure to theories of teaching and learning, consciously formulate personal philosophies about teaching. For many fellows, the core of their emerging teaching philosophies is a humanism that emphasizes appreciation of student differences, interest in listening to students, and a greater commitment to fostering the process of students' intellectual growth than to dispensing knowledge.

---

*From 1974 through 1988, the period of Austin's study, 568 junior, non-tenured faculty from 30 research universities participated in the Lilly Endowment Teaching Fellows Program. Of those for whom mailing addresses could be located, the researcher received responses, in one form or another (comprehensive written survey, brief telephone survey, short written survey), from 412 people, or 86 percent. Data also were obtained from participating universities' program directors, associate directors, department chairs of fellows, and other university administrators. The methods for gathering data included reviewing archival materials and conducting written and telephone surveys, interviews, and case studies. For more information about the study methodology, see Austin 1992b, pp. 88-92.

*Past fellows have reported that they became more attentive
to students' learning needs; more sensitive to such barriers
as learning disabilities, anxiety, and challenges associated
with English as a second language; and more careful about
helping students link theoretical concepts and practical problems. This heightened sensitivity to students' diverse needs
and challenges, coupled with exploration of teaching and
learning theory, often causes fellows to cultivate new
approaches to their teaching. Through group meetings and
individual projects, fellows learn about creative teaching
methods—the use of computers, games, simulations, and
cooperative learning, for example—and often develop new
instructional materials* (1992a, p. 80).

Despite the improved teaching of these junior faculty from
research universities, success has not come without its costs.
As Austin observes, some faculty have indicated that "the fellowship diverted time from research and signaled a strong
interest in teaching—both perceived to be negative considerations in tenure review [and] frustration with the time that
both excellence in research and teaching requires" (1992b,
p. 89).

And apparent success notwithstanding, Austin has issued
three caveats with respect to overgeneralizing the findings
(1992b, p. 92). She explains:

*First, the teaching fellowship is just one element in the
careers of the participants; thus its impact is difficult to iso-
late. Probably most who become fellows already have considerable interest in teaching and also participate in other
faculty and instructional development activities. Second,
since participants invested much time and effort into the
program, they might overemphasize its benefits and effects
to justify their commitment. Third, a comparison of fellows
and nonfellows' career experiences and teaching-related
attitudes and values would have been valuable in identifying effects unique to the fellowship, but it was not possible
given the time constraints of the study.*

Officials affiliated with and external reviewers of the New Jersey Master Faculty Program and its successor, Partners in
Learning, also have told us a great deal about how teaching
improves when faculty take part in formative peer evaluation.

According to the program manual:

> *Through the observation process, paired faculty are often exposed to teaching styles quite different from their own. On a superficial level, the observers might focus on techniques that they could apply to their own classrooms. On a deeper level, the ongoing experience may trigger a self-examination that can lead to growth and change more profound than any classroom technique* (NJICTL 1991, p. 9).

Steven Golin, at one time the state program director, explains how students, through interviews with faculty, have motivated professors to improve their teaching:

> *As students reflect on their experience, or explain how they construct meaning, we listen, or ask questions. The roles are reversed: They teach, we take notes. Beyond anything the students say—and they are surprisingly articulate about the priorities, their experiences, and their strategies—the process of listening attentively to them affects most of us deeply. Enjoying their active participation and excited by the view from below, we look for ways to bring some of that excitement and enjoyment into the classroom. The new relationship with students whom we interview, like the relationship with our partner, transforms our attitude toward teaching and learning* (1990, p. 10).

An early external program review has also reported on improvement in teaching:

> *Many changes in techniques and procedures occurred as early as the first semester. Beyond teaching techniques, however, faculty have gained new insights into the learning and teaching process. Several essays [written by program participants] reflected the importance of being demanding yet caring; connecting with and supporting each student. This invitational approach to teaching, welcoming students to become active participants, can make a difference* (Rice and Cheldelin 1989, pp. 21-22).

Rice and Cheldelin also note that "through the various components of the program, faculty have learned a great deal about themselves. Not only are they becoming more sensitive

and effective in dealing with the developmental tasks confronting students, they are discovering a renewed enthusiasm—even passion—for teaching as a vocation" (p. 23).
On balance, there seems to be a basis for claims that formative peer evaluation is successful in improving teaching. More generally, as Erickson and Erickson indicate, faculty believe that such programs are "useful and well worth the time and effort, and that it results in significant, positive, and lasting changes in their classroom teaching skill performance" (1979, p. 683). It should be obvious, however, that further rigorous study of existing programs is needed before definitive conclusions about program success can be made.

Improvement in Student Learning

It is almost unanimously assumed that the true measure of successful teaching is the quantity and quality of student learning. By extrapolation, it often is assumed that the primary goal of formative evaluation of instruction is to facilitate improvements in student learning. While commendable in principle, scholars are quick to point to difficulties involved in using student learning as a criterion in assessing teacher performance and instructional improvement programs. Concerns of this type are expressed in various ways.

Scholars emphasize that many factors contribute to, and detract from, student learning, and only one of these factors is teacher performance. Dennis, for example, notes that:

The effectiveness of a teacher is related to a host of student, environmental, social and sexual characteristics. [These factors] include social-economic status, educational level of parents, maturity level of students, the differing experiences among ethnic groups, peer pressures, and so on (1976, p. 440).

Seldin adds that:

The quantity and quality of student learning are also affected by the student's general academic ability, motivation to learn, organizing and writing ability on exams, skill in multiple-choice exams, study habits, and image, favorable or unfavorable, in the professor's mind. Each factor affects student achievement (1984, p. 122).

There are, no doubt, other factors that also affect student learning.

With factors in mind such as those mentioned above, Bulcock concludes that, among teachers,

> *Efforts to measure teaching effectiveness on the basis of its impact on student learning is unpopular. This is because most teachers recognize that student learning is a multi-causal activity, and that many significant factors . . . fall well outside the control of the teacher. Thus, to hold teachers responsible for the learning behaviors of their students is unreasonable* (1984, p. 8).

Elaborating on the theme that much of what students learn lies outside of the teacher's purview, Menges writes:

> *Although most teaching occurs in the classroom, most learning does not. A great deal of learning occurs out of the presence of the teacher. Learning may occur in libraries, laboratories, studios, study rooms, and living areas. Indeed, learning may occur in any setting where learners encounter the subject matter for study.*
>
> *The job of the teacher is to be cognizant of all those settings, using them to shape an environment conducive to learning. The essence of teaching is the creation of situations in which appropriate learning occurs; shaping those situations is what successful teachers have learned to do effectively* (1990, p. 107).

Scholars sometimes argue specifically that test performance and other student products should be used as measures of teacher competence. Some of the difficulties in using these materials have been posed as rhetorical questions by Chickering:

> *Do we assess the amount of learning that occurs among students, the "value added" in knowledge, competence, and personal development that occurs in our courses? Do we evaluate the degree to which knowledge and competence demonstrated at the end of a course or the gains that have occurred are retained? For how long? A semester? A year? Until graduation? Beyond graduation? What are reasonable*

expectations concerning the amount of learning or gain
that might occur in a single course? And how do these expec-
tations need to vary given the prior ability, knowledge, com-
petence, and experiences of students? Is a large gain by a
relatively poor student to be given more weight than a small
gain by a very bright, well-prepared student? (1984, p. 93)

Stated simply, "even when learning outcome information is
available for a particular course, we may be unable to determine what part of the outcome should be attributed to that
particular teacher and course" (Menges 1990, p. 112).

And with respect to using student outcome measures for
evaluating instructional development efforts, Erickson and
Erickson conclude:

It is difficult to deny the attractiveness of student learning
gains as criteria for judging teaching improvement services,
but we may have to defer their use as major criteria until
more practical and powerful evaluation methodologies are
available for dealing with the confounding influences of
textbooks and peers (1979, p. 671).

In conclusion, Cross' observations about teaching and learning seem especially apt:

The ultimate criterion of effective teaching is effective learn-
ing. There is simply no other reason for teaching. But learn-
ing probably depends more on the behavior *of students than*
on the performance *of the teacher. . . . Good teaching is not*
so much a performing act as an evocative process. The pur-
pose is to involve students actively in their own learning and
to elicit from them their best learning performance (emphasis hers) (1991, p. 20).

If Cross' notions about teaching and learning are to be incor-
porated into instructional development programs in general
and formative peer evaluation in particular, faculty, administrators, and teaching consultants will have to look at teaching
in ways to which many of them are unaccustomed. But by
examining teaching from this broader perspective, evaluators
may be able to reach the essence, nuance, and substance of
this complex professional role.

Improvement in Faculty Morale and Collegiality

It seems obvious that the purposes for which evaluation is carried out would affect faculty morale and collegiality in different ways. On one hand, researchers have found that voluntary faculty involvement in *formative* evaluation of teaching usually affects faculty morale and the collegial climate of the institution positively (Austin 1992a, 1992b; Carton 1988; Cross 1986; Edwards 1974; Freer and Dawson 1985; Heller 1989; Katz and Henry 1988; Menges 1985, 1987; Roper, Deal, and Dornbusch 1976; Shatzky and Silberman 1986; Skoog 1980; Sorcinelli 1984). On the other, they generally have agreed that peer review in the process of *summative* evaluation affects morale and collegiality negatively (Brandenburg, Braskamp, and Ory 1979; Braskamp 1978; Centra 1993; Gunn 1982; McIntyre 1978; Sorcinelli 1984).

Despite researchers' findings that morale and collegiality will be improved by faculty participation in formative peer evaluation, many faculty apparently are unconvinced. Only about 23 percent of faculty from independent colleges and universities surveyed believe morale would be improved, and approximately 43 percent believe the collegial climate of the institution would be enhanced (Keig 1991). In another study, Britt has found that about half of respondents did not believe faculty morale would be lowered, but the remainder have expressed the opposite view or were not sure (1982). While the attitudes of faculty are mixed on these issues, it seems clear that proponents of formative peer evaluation will have to "sell" the benefits of this form of instructional improvement to a skeptical faculty. The following research findings and testimonials are perhaps a place to start.

Researchers and faculty members themselves have found that participation in formative peer evaluation has improved the morale of both senior and junior faculty. From one study, Heller has concluded:

> *Using teachers in a peer supervision role is linked to their personal growth, their sense of collegiality, and to improved instructional practices—all of which contribute to higher morale, greater job satisfaction, improved school climate, and ultimately higher student achievement* (1989, p. 11).

From his experience as a participant in a program of formative peer evaluation, a full professor at a research university notes:

*To me the project was the balm of Gilead; nothing less. For,
if I read Erik Erikson correctly, the crisis that a full tenured
professor of fifty might face originates in the internal conflict between impulses to remain generative, productive, or
creative and impulses to stagnate, wither, and dissolve. . . .*

*So to a professor in his fifties, a personal invitation seriously
to reconsider his teaching is an invitation to his internal
forces of generativity to take heart. Implied in the invitation
was the suggestion that what had been learned in my private
experience in years of classroom teaching was worthy of
public examination. The invitation suggested that work in
one's classroom and one's thoughts about it deserved the
attention of the uppermost echelons of the campus; that as
an individual the professor in the classroom was worth
training and retraining; that there was a belief in the possibility of training him and in the value of what he had
already learned. Most importantly the project implied that
the students we work with require our serious attention,
that there is much that we have to learn about them, and
that we have to discover them if we are to teach them. What
could be more heartening? What could resonate with one's
personal commitments more? To understand even more
fully why I should have been enthusiastic about the project
we should also consider that a tenured full professor has
nothing to lose. His position in the university is secure. By
honing his skills in teaching, the senior full professor adds
to the areas in which he can exercise leadership* (Carton
1988, pp. 54-55).

Junior faculty taking part in the Lilly Teaching Fellows Program, formative peer evaluation projects put into place at
research universities, also have found that morale and collegiality improved from their involvement. As Austin reports:

*Greater self-confidence, self-esteem, and morale have been
important consequences of the fellowship, identified both
in self-reports by fellows and in observations by department
chairs, mentors, and program directors. Some reported that
the program strengthened fellows' confidence that they could
handle the multiple pressures of career and family, and
could balance teaching and research responsibilities. Others
appreciated the fellowship experience as a positive part of*

*the transition from graduate student to faculty member,
from uncertainty to confidence. . . . The feeling that the
university had invested in them and cared about their work
and careers enhanced confidence and morale for some*
(1992b, p. 97).

Scholars also address more specifically how collegiality has
been affected by participation in formative peer review. Skoog
concludes that, through such professional activity,

*Faculty members acquire knowledge, insights, and strategies
useful for self-supervision and self-improvement. Also, as
a team works together, supportive relationships are estab-
lished and discussions concerning teaching become more
common, lengthy, and sophisticated. Ownership of common
and unique teaching problems is acknowledged more
openly. Increased satisfaction and pride in teaching can
result* (1980, p. 24).

Galm has observed that senior faculty often are highly skeptical—even cynical—about programs of instructional improvement (1985). He reports, however, on how the collegiality
of senior English faculty improved by participating in a program of peer review designed by and for themselves, noting
that:

*Working with this post-tenure study group, I got a completely
different sense of my department, one that was in my bones
but, because of the distractions of student complaints, not
always in my head. I experienced the power of eight teachers
and colleagues, a solid core of a permanent faculty of fifty,
showing their concern for teaching and demonstrating their
accumulated skill. It was awesome, and a fine corrective
for any department chair who may have become cynical
or have lost insight of the great faculty power in his or her
department* (p. 67).

While scholars, researchers, and participants alike agree that
participating in programs of formative peer evaluation can
lead to improved morale and collegiality, they also have indicated that the most successful programs involve the faculty
in program planning and implementation, rely on voluntary
participation, and have the unconditional support of top-level

administrators. Without the unqualified backing of the faculty and of influential administrators, instructional improvement programs are not likely to sustain themselves for any substantial length of time.

Improvement in the Tenure Success of Junior Faculty

Proponents of formative peer evaluation of teaching would probably like to believe that participating in it would improve the tenure success of junior faculty. Evidence supporting this proposition is, at this time, inconclusive, and the literature on the topic is scanty.

Austin has found that 27 percent of faculty who participated in the Lilly Teaching Fellows Program as junior faculty at research universities believed it had helped them achieve tenure, but 34 percent thought it had no effect (1992b). Austin explains that:

Those who perceived the fellowship as having a positive effect on tenure gave several reasons: they enhanced their teaching skills and thus their credentials; through fellows' meetings, they learned about the tenure process; and their project work contributed to their publishing record. Also, according to some senior faculty, department chairs, and deans, selection as a teaching fellow appears on a vita as a prestigious award.

Austin says that those who indicated that participation had little effect in the tenure decision believe that:

Attention to teaching is personally gratifying and typically does not hurt tenure credentials unless it is offered as a substitute for research activity; but their responses clearly indicate that the quality and quantity of research is the primary (some would say sole) factor considered in a tenure decision. While department chairs and administrators interviewed typically praised the fellowship experience and saw it as a positive addition to the tenure dossier, they simultaneously acknowledged a continuing strong emphasis on research productivity in tenure decisions (1992b, p. 98).

At research universities, at least, participation in programs of instructional improvement has had, apparently, little effect in achieving tenure. Whether the same conclusion would

Studies also appear to show that faculty morale and collegiality improve when faculty are involved in formative peer evaluation.

apply to other types of colleges and universities remains unexamined, although 60 percent of faculty at independent colleges and universities in a Midwestern state believe that junior faculty involving themselves in formative peer evaluation would enhance their tenure chances (Keig 1991).

Studies seem to indicate not only *that* but *how* teaching is improved when faculty avail themselves of instructional development programs in which they work collaboratively to improve teaching. Studies also appear to show that faculty morale and collegiality improve when faculty are involved in formative peer evaluation. While student learning may improve when faculty take part in such programs, that is a difficult claim to substantiate, since many variables affect student learning. At this time, there is not enough evidence to suggest that the tenure status of junior faculty is enhanced when they have participated in formative peer assessment.

Further research is needed with respect to faculty participation in formative peer evaluation and the purported benefits of this involvement. There is also a need for study of how formative peer review is or is not related to life stage and career stage theories.

RECOMMENDATIONS AND CONCLUSIONS

We have learned many lessons from our review of the literature on formative peer evaluation of college teaching. First, we have found compelling the rationales for comprehensive faculty evaluation, formative evaluation apart from summative evaluation, and peer review as part of the formative evaluation process. Second, we have learned there are roles in faculty assessment that colleagues can perform with distinction but also have learned there are roles they are less-suited to perform. At the same time, we have discovered that students, academic administrators, and teaching consultants have parts to play, each constituency having its own areas of strengths and limitations. Third, we have found there are several methods of assessment faculty can use to critique the teaching of colleagues. We have discussed the merits of five of these methods but acknowledge there may be other methods that also might be employed.

Fourth, we have discovered and are discouraged by the fact that faculty are reluctant to involve themselves in programs of instructional improvement, in part because they are skeptical about its value, because they are fearful of the process, and probably also because the academy's rewards and incentives often fail to support such activity. We believe that the academic community will have to reconsider some of its priorities if faculty are going to be willing to commit time and energy to instructional improvement programs. That said, we are heartened to find there are ways to enhance the likelihood of faculty participation in such programs.

Fifth, we are convinced that individual faculty, students, and colleges and universities will benefit from faculty participation in formative evaluation. Sixth, we have learned there is much yet to be learned about formative peer evaluation.

Recommendations

As we read and thought about formative peer evaluation of teaching; examined reports describing the nature, strengths, and weaknesses of program examples; and reviewed the limited critical research on the effectiveness of instructional improvement, certain themes have recurred often enough for us to gain a sense of what successful programs are. The following recommendations are, for the most part, general and broad-based; other, more specific recommendations have been presented in preceding sections of the report.

1. Faculty evaluation should include largely separate formative and summative tracks. Summative evaluation, including rigorous quantitative and qualitative data-gathering and analysis, is essential for maintaining the academy's integrity; formative evaluation, including equally rigorous descriptive strategies, along with ample feedback and opportunities for practice and coaching, is necessary for improving teaching.

Since there apparently is little correlation between summative evaluation and instructional improvement, strategies that actually promote better teaching must be identified and put into practice. We believe that instructional development requires a distinctly different approach to evaluation than the practices normally used for making personnel decisions. We are convinced that a truly comprehensive program of evaluation must include two parallel, essentially separate tracks: summative for decisions regarding reappointment, promotion, tenure and compensation; formative for instructional improvement (and, if desired, for assistance with scholarship and service). Our conception of these two forms of evaluation is presented as Figure 7.

FIGURE 7

Comprehensive College Faculty Evaluation

Formative Evaluation			Summative Evaluation
Descriptive Analysis of and Assistance With			A Global Judgment of
Teaching	Scholarship	Service	Teaching, Scholarship, and Service

Critics of higher education frequently remind us that college teaching needs to be taken more seriously since it is, in fact, "the business of the business." Unless faculty intrinsically are motivated by their teaching responsibilities—in addition to scholarship and service—or are fascinated with "tinkering with teaching," assuming they know how to fix what isn't working, ways must be found to make instructional development activities attractive and useful to them. While these strategies may have to include changes in the institution's reward structure, it may be just as important to look for approaches that faculty needing and seeking help in improving their teaching find intellectually engaging.

2. Formative evaluation should include nonjudgmental descriptions of faculty members' teaching by colleagues, academic administrators, and, where available, teaching consultants as well as students; each of these constituencies should be asked for data only in areas in which the constituency is qualified to provide such data.

We believe that, since teaching is such a complex activity, it is unlikely any individual or group can accurately assess the full range of a faculty member's teaching behaviors. For that reason, we present a conception of instructional development involving data gathering and analysis by faculty colleagues, academic administrators, teaching consultants, students, and—ultimately—the professor's self-assessment of his or her teaching. In our *Model for the Formative Evaluation of Teaching* (Figure 8), bold outlining and connecting lines indicate what we consider primary sources in the *formative* evaluation of *teaching;* lighter outlining and linkages indicate secondary sources. The importance of these sources probably would be quite different in the formative evaluation of research and service and in the summative evaluation of professional performance.

Students are accurate and reliable providers of information about many presentational aspects of teaching but are less able to assess an instructor's expertise in content knowledge, the quality of course content, and student outcomes. The instructor's knowledge of subject matter, course content, the relationship of content in one course to other courses, and student achievement should be assessed by colleagues, academic administrators, and/or teaching consultants. If faculty are to make accurate self-assessments of their teaching, they must receive information that is sensible and valid.

3. Faculty should be encouraged to take part in year-long programs of formative peer review of teaching every four or five years over the course of their teaching careers; that encouragement needs to come from administrators and senior faculty.

FIGURE 8

A Model for Formative Evaluation of Teaching

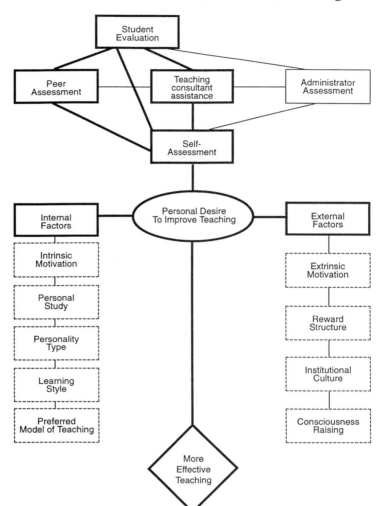

Fruitful instructional improvement programs require substantial time commitments from and effort of participants, not short-term "quick fixes" or onetime "shots." To have a reasonable chance of improving performance, collaborative relationships should extend beyond a single term of instruction and involve periodic formative peer review, not just committee action when personnel decisions are pending.

Yet, time is a precious commodity, so there may be limits to what is productive. In advocating that faculty participate in intense programs of formative peer evaluation every four or five years, we believe we are consistent with Brinko's (1993) finding that "feedback is more effective when given frequently, but not excessively" (p. 585).

4. Faculty should take leadership in the design and implementation of evaluation programs to improve teaching. Although this would seem to go without saying, it is imperative that for such programs to be effective, they must come from the faculty. The history and traditions of faculty governance of matters pertaining to curriculum and instruction require that developmental initiatives like this be handled similarly.

To ignore this reality is to risk either outright faculty rejection and nonparticipation or a cool, skeptical reception that can slow down, draw out, and enervate any administration-imposed plan. This is not to say that there is no important role for the administration to play—quite the contrary. The support of the administration is critical to the success of such programs insofar as they provide the incentives and rewards that underscore the importance of the activity in the mission and life of the institution.

5. Peer participation in formative evaluation involves the assessment of several aspects of teaching; peers should be trained in the skills needed to conduct these assessments.

Faculty must be knowledgeable in a number of areas when assisting in the improvement of their peers' teaching. As elaborated on in the section on faculty roles, these areas each have unique characteristics and skills associated with them. To be really helpful to peers, faculty who would be involved in formative evaluation should be trained in what to look for and how to assist.

It may be assumed that because one has been teaching for a long time, this would not be necessary. While it is true that one accumulates experience and a certain folk wisdom about teaching in one's field (Shulman acknowledges this in his category "pedagogical content knowledge"), it is important to test these assumptions against what has been learned in recent years from cognitive and developmental psychology. The line between experiential wisdom and mythology can blur. Addressing this in the context of training for assessment of specific areas of teaching can help keep these predispositions in perspective.

6. The involvement of peers in the formative evaluation of teaching should be guided by expertise from appropriate areas of the knowledge base of teaching; at the same time, care must be taken to minimize potential problems that can derive from those same individuals' involvement in summative evaluation.

The issue at the heart of this recommendation is the potential problem presented by a peer participating in formative evaluation and later serving in a judgmental role for promotion or tenure decisions. The underlying assumption is that the two processes must occur separately and that, ideally, no one should be part of both processes as an evaluator. This must be so, the argument continues, because it is not possible to be objective when one has been part of the early process of observing and contributing to the "product" in development. In such a case, the "formative atmosphere" may be tainted by the foreshadowing of judgment to come—that any suggestions offered to the faculty member may be interpreted as directives, possibly inhibiting the development of unique strengths or ideas in the interest of conformity and survival.

This may be an academic freedom question in its *lernfreiheit* aspect. This concern may be compounded by the fact that in this time of increasing specialization and, some would say, fragmentation, the number of faculty with the background to comment upon the content aspects of a colleague's teaching is limited; this would be particularly true of smaller liberal arts colleges with one- or two-person departments.

There are three considerations that guide our recommendation in this area. First, we suggest drawing on concepts outlined and described in Shulman's (1987) knowledge and teaching construct, discussed in the introduction of this report. By broadening the resources brought to bear in formative evaluation, the faculty member receiving this input can benefit from multiple points of view and expertise that rarely resides solely in one person. And since some of these areas are outside content specialization, the door is opened to faculty outside of one's field. A number of universities around the country have teaching-enhancement centers with consultants and faculty fellows who can help with particular aspects of the framework outlined by Shulman.

The second consideration is philosophical. We are among the increasing number of those who believe that one cannot separate fact from value—that we are all participants in inquiry and must take into account the ontological and epistemological constructs and methodological approaches that together constitute our point of view.

The third consideration guiding this recommendation is that in the end, we must rely upon the integrity and "good faith" of the faculty. The tradition of faculty governance of their own affairs is long and, for the most part, distinguished. This is but another area in which faculty must be just and caring.

7. **Formative peer evaluation should include direct classroom observation, videotaping of classes, evaluation of course materials, assessment of instructor evaluations of the academic work of students, and analysis of teaching portfolios. In this process, the methods should probably be used in combination, not as independent entities.**

We are convinced that faculty are qualified to assess many aspects of colleagues' teaching and capable of assisting peers in improving their teaching. To maximize the benefits of formative peer assessment, we believe that evaluators should avail themselves not only of the methods already mentioned, but also their abilities to interpret student ratings of courses and instructors—and relevant data from other sources—and conduct interviews with students and colleagues with an eye toward examining relationships between teaching strategies and student learning. Used together, these approaches can provide significant detail about various points of the teaching-learning process: where a teacher is preparing to teach the course, where a teacher and his or her students are involved in and reacting to the process, and where a teacher evaluates students' academic work, provides feedback to students and attempts to motivate them, and considers future versions of the course.

a. Peer observation should be an important component of formative evaluation of teaching; however, it should not be the only component.

Colleagues can observe a peer's class from different vantage points than students and other constituencies. Because most students attend class more regularly than peer observers, students probably are the most qualified observers of a teacher's presentational skills. On the other hand, faculty no doubt are much more capable in examining the relationships between the nature of the content and delivery and between the content of one course and other courses in the curriculum.

We believe that formative peer evaluation and peer observation too often are considered synonymous entities. We think that formative peer evaluation should be more comprehensive, including a number of methods of assessment besides peer observation.

b. The videotaping of classes and video playback/ feedback should be an integral component of formative peer evaluation of teaching. It should be employed for what it can contribute in its own right, not viewed simply as an alternative to direct classroom observation.

Though probably the most self-confrontational of the formative evaluation methods, video playback/feedback should be used in conjunction with other methods of formative evaluation, not avoided. To reduce its often stressful and threatening nature, we suggest that an instructor view tapes of his or her classes with a supportive colleague or teaching consultant who has been trained in how to interpret what has been recorded. Good consultation skills are required to reinforce positive aspects and to diffuse negative reactions that can come from viewing a recorded performance that is deemed less than satisfactory.

c. Formative peer evaluation should include examination of course syllabi, readings, teacher-made tests, teacher-designed papers, projects, presentations, and other assigned work; professors should be encouraged to ask for feedback from colleagues

**on course materials as they would on manuscripts
planned for publication.**

Peer evaluation of course materials expands the range of
teacher attitudes, behaviors, and competencies that should
be reviewed. Making course materials available to colleagues
is a way for faculty to demonstrate the quality of course content and its relationship to the academic work required of
students.

Colleagues from the same field of study or from closely
related fields are especially well-qualified to assess the appropriateness of materials in relation to particular courses and
groups of students and in context of departmental and college
curricula. Faculty also are better able than any other constituency to look at relationships between course materials and
teaching strategies. We believe that peer evaluation of course
materials should become a commonplace practice in formative peer evaluation.

> *Faculty also
> are better able
> than any other
> constituency
> to look at
> relationships
> between
> course
> materials and
> teaching
> strategies.*

   **d. Peer assessment of instructor evaluations of the
   academic work of students should occur as a corollary to peer evaluation of course materials.**

Peer review of instructor evaluations of students' academic
work can reveal pertinent information about a teacher's commitment to teaching. A faculty member's practices in evaluating tests, papers, projects, presentations, and other assignments can tell reviewers much about the professor's attitudes
toward students, especially about how feedback on written
work is used as a motivator. Peer review of instructor evaluations of students' work should be used to complement what
is learned from other methods of formative evaluation. We
believe that such assessment should be used much more
extensively in formative evaluation.

   **e. The teaching portfolio should be used for self-
   assessment and formative peer evaluation of teaching; its use should not be restricted to documenting
   performance for personnel decision making.**

The teaching portfolio is an opportunity for faculty to present an almost limitless array of materials that document their
teaching. When the purpose of a portfolio is instructional
improvement, faculty should be encouraged to include a
representative sample of materials, so that a peer reviewer
can see what an instructor's typical teaching is like.

The teaching portfolio appears to be a promising means
for evaluating teaching. Its potential for improving teaching

should be exploited.

8. Institutional rewards and incentives should be structured so as to demonstrate to faculty that participation in programs of formative peer evaluation to improve teaching is truly valued.

In the section on disincentives, we have outlined several factors that may attenuate faculty participation in programs of this type. Despite the renewed call for an emphasis on teaching as "the business of the business," the implicit message remains—publish. As it has been said, "You have to write to stay (to get tenured and promoted) and you have to write to leave (to be marketable across "the industry"). The principal variable here, we believe, is time. If faculty are made to feel that they can invest the time, and it will take time, and that it will not come at the expense of their professional status, then the ground is prepared for their participation.

We would suggest going a step further, however. Not only should the implicit threat of punishment be removed, but incentives and rewards to participate should be introduced. All across the country, at the institutional level, systems of financial grants and release time are in place encouraging faculty to conduct research and to write. A simple measure to address this recommendation would be to set alongside these research awards similar awards for those who would devote time to training for and participating in formative peer evaluation. The most effective approach to this significant problem, we believe, would be more thorough attention given to the multiple disincentives discussed in the text of this report. A systemic as well as a systematic program rewarding the improvement of teaching has the best chance, we believe, to realize the benefits that we have discussed in the section on personal and institutional benefits. We believe that most faculty are essentially magnanimous and that given a conducive atmosphere that encourages and rewards, rather than punishes, they will be helpful.

In this connection, we further suggest that such comprehensive programs take into account faculty members' career and life stages. There should be special incentives and rewards for the young assistant professor as well as the senior full professor. There should be recognition of evolving personal and developmental changes that can occur over time, since most of us change in our interests and attitudes over the course of our careers. Incentives and rewards should take into account these dimensions of our lives as whole people as well.

9. Research should proceed along several potentially lucrative lines.

First, research needs to be performed about the interaction of variables affecting formative peer evaluation in specific institutional contexts. While we purport to know general conditions that are required for such programs to succeed, differences among institutions with regard to governance traditions, collective bargaining, and other variables need to be investigated for what they contribute to successful or unsuccessful implementation.

Second, research is needed to tie evaluation to motivational theory. This is to add support to a similar call from Blackburn and others (1991). While we can speak in broad terms about motivation to participate in and to support programs to improve teaching, we need to speak more specifically about how motivation comes into play.

Third, we believe there is a need to document and more widely report the experiences with formative evaluation programs where they exist, regardless of whether they are succeeding. There is a paucity of such reporting in the literature, as our section on program examples should indicate. There may be an opportunity here for a national higher education organization to facilitate such an effort through conferences, a clearinghouse, or use of the Internet. Systematic empirical and ethnographic research of initiatives could contribute much to our understanding as well.

Conclusions

No longer are the outcries for reform of higher education emanating solely from outside the academy. In fact, some of the most strident criticism—as well as the most thoughtful comments on improving college teaching—are coming from the ranks of the professoriate.

Faculty understand, perhaps better than anyone else, that improving the quality of teaching is complicated by many factors, all of which enter into their discussions on how it can be accomplished. Not the least of these factors is the epistemological issue of what "effective teaching" is. In a sense, lack of agreement on this issue supports a flexible, formative approach to assessment, one in which the faculty play principal roles. From years of experience as students and teachers, they know that successful teachers demonstrate not only command of subject matter but also knowledge of teaching strategies and learning theories, commitment to the intellectual and personal development of their students, awareness of the complex contexts in which instruction occurs, and concern about their colleagues' performance. Perhaps more effectively than any other of the academy's constituencies, they can describe and analyze their peers' teaching and assist them in improving this aspect of professional performance.

We believe that formative peer evaluation is a promising method in which faculty can work cooperatively to improve teaching. We are convinced the time has come for the academic community to look seriously at its potential, for faculty and administrators to collaborate in developing and implementing this form of instructional improvement, and for researchers to evaluate the results in appropriately rigorous ways.

REFERENCES

The Educational Resources Information Center (ERIC) Clearinghouse
on Higher Education abstracts and indexes the current literature on
higher education for inclusion in ERIC's data base and announce-
ment in ERIC's monthly bibliographic journal, *Resources in Education* (RIE). Most of these publications are available through the
ERIC Document Reproduction Service (EDRS). For publications cited
in this bibliography that are available from EDRS, ordering number
and price code are included. Readers who wish to order a publication should write to the ERIC Document Reproduction Service,
7420 Fullerton Rd., Suite 110, Springfield, VA 22153-2852. (Phone
orders with VISA or MasterCard are taken at 800-443-ERIC or
703-440-1400.) When ordering, please specify the document (ED)
number. Documents are available as noted in microfiche (MF) and
paper copy (PC). If you have the price code ready when you call
EDRS, an exact price can be quoted. The last page of the latest issue
of *Resources in Education* also has the current cost, listed by code.

Abraham, M.R., and D.H. Ost. 1978. "Improving Teaching Through
Formative Evaluation." *Journal of College Science Teaching* 7:
227-29.

Abrami, P.C. 1985. "Dimensions of Effective College Instruction."
Review of Higher Education 8: 211-28.

Aleamoni, L.M. 1981. *Standards for Evaluation of Instruction.* Note
to the Faculty, No. 11. Tucson: University of Arizona Institutional
Research and Development.

————. 1984. *Peer Evaluation.* Note to the Faculty, No. 15. Tucson:
University of Arizona Institutional Research and Development.

————. 1987. "Some Practical Approaches for Faculty and Administrators." In *Techniques for Evaluating and Improving Teaching,*
edited by L.M. Aleamoni. New Directions for Teaching and Learning
No. 31. San Francisco: Jossey-Bass.

Aleamoni, L.M., and M. Yimer. 1973. "An Investigation of the Relationship Between Colleague Rating, Student Rating, Research Productivity, and Academic Rank in Rating Instructional Effectiveness."
Journal of Educational Psychology 64(3): 274-77.

American Association for Higher Education. 1994. "'Peer Review of
Teaching' Initiative." *AAHE Bulletin* 46(10): 16+.

Anderson, E., ed. 1993. *Campus Use of the Teaching Portfolio: 25
Profiles.* Washington, D.C.: American Association for Higher
Education.

Angelo, T.A. 1989. "Faculty Development for Learning." In *To Improve
The Academy,* edited by S. Kahn. Stillwater, Okla.: New Forums
Press.

————. 1993. "A 'Teacher's Dozen': Fourteen General, Research-
Based Principles for Improving Higher Learning in Our Classrooms." *AAHE Bulletin* 45(8): 3-7+.

Arden, E. Summer 1989. "Who Should Judge the Faculty?" *The College Board Review:* 37-39.

Arreola, R.A. 1984. "Evaluation of Faculty Performance: Key Issues." In *Changing Practices in Faculty Evaluation*, by P. Seldin. San Francisco: Jossey-Bass.

Arubayi, E.A. 1987. "Improvement of Instruction and Teacher Effectiveness: Are Student Ratings Reliable and Valid?" *Higher Education* 16: 267-78.

Ashford, S.J., and L.L. Cummings. 1983. "Feedback as an Individual Resource: Personal Strategies of Creating Information." *Organizational Behavior and Human Performance* 32: 370-98.

Astin, A.W., and C.B.T. Lee. 1966. "Current Practices in the Evaluation and Training of College Teachers." *Educational Record* 47: 361-75.

Aubrecht, J.D. 1984. "Better Faculty Evaluation Systems." In *Changing Practices in Faculty Evaluation*, by P. Seldin. San Francisco: Jossey-Bass.

Austin, A.E. 1990a. "Supporting the Professor as Teacher: An Evaluation Study of the Lilly Teaching Fellows Program." Paper presented at the 15th annual meeting of the American Association for the Study of Higher Education, Portland, Ore. ED 232 554. 38 pp. MF-01; PC-02.

―――. 1990b. *"To Leave an Indelible Mark: Encouraging Good Teaching in Research Universities Through Faculty Development: A Study of the Lilly Endowment's Teaching Fellows Program, 1974-1988."* Nashville, Tenn.: Peabody College, Vanderbilt University.

―――. 1992a. "Supporting Junior Faculty Through a Teaching Fellows Program." In *Developing New and Junior Faculty*, edited by M.D. Sorcinelli and A.E. Austin. New Directions for Teaching and Learning No. 50. San Francisco: Jossey-Bass.

―――. 1992b. "Supporting the Professor as Teacher: The Lilly Teaching Fellows Program." *Review of Higher Education* 16: 85-106.

Austin, A.E., and R.G. Baldwin. 1991. *Faculty Collaboration: Enhancing the Quality of Scholarship and Teaching.* ASHE-ERIC Higher Education Report No. 7. Washington, D.C.: Association for the Study of Higher Education. ED 346 805. 138 pp. MF-01; PC-06.

Baldwin, R.G.. 1979. "Adult and Career Development: What Are the Implications for Faculty?" In *Current Issues in Higher Education*, edited by R. Edgerton. Washington, D.C.: American Association for Higher Education.

―――. March/April 1990. "Faculty Vitality Beyond the Research University." *Journal of Higher Education* 61: 160-80.

Baldwin, R.G., and R.T. Blackburn. November/December 1981. "The Academic Career as a Developmental Process." *Journal of Higher Education* 52: 598-614.

Ballard, M.J., J. Reardon, and L. Nelson. 1976. "Student and Peer Ratings of Faculty." *Teaching of Psychology* 3: 88-91.

Batista, E.E. 1976. "The Place of Colleague Evaluation in the Appraisal of College Teaching: A Review of the Literature." *Research in Higher Education* 4: 257-71.

Bell, M.E., E.C. Dobson, and J.M. Gram. Fall 1977. "Peer Evaluation As a Method of Faculty Development." *Journal of the College and University Personnel Administration* 28: 15-17.

Bennett, W.E. 1987. "Small Group Instructional Diagnosis: A Dialogic Approach to Instructional Improvement for Tenured Faculty." *The Journal of Staff, Program, and Organizational Development* 5(3): 100-04.

Bergman, J. 1979. "The Effectiveness of Peer Ratings at the University Level." *Journal of Teaching and Learning* 4(3): 34-37.

———. 1980. "Peer Evaluation of University Faculty." *College Student Journal* (monograph ed.) 14(3, Pt. II): 1-21.

Bergquist, W. 1979. "The Liberal Arts College." In *Designing Teaching Improvement Programs*, edited by J. Lindquist. Washington, D.C.: Council for the Advancement of Small Colleges.

Bergquist, W.H., and S.R. Phillips. 1975. *A Handbook for Faculty Development.* New York: Danville.

Bess, J.L., ed. 1982. *Motivating Professors to Teach Effectively.* San Francisco: Jossey-Bass.

Blackburn, R.T., and M.T. Clark. 1975. "An Assessment of Faculty Performance: Some Correlates Between Administrator, Colleague, Student, and Self-Ratings. *Sociology of Education* 48: 342-56.

Blackburn, R.J., J.H. Lawrence, J.P. Bieber, and L. Trautvetter. 1991. "Faculty At Work: Focus On Teaching." *Research in Higher Education* 32: 363-81.

Boyer, E.L. 1987. *College: The Undergraduate Experience in America.* New York: Harper & Row.

Brandenburg, D.C., L.A. Braskamp, and J.C. Ory. Winter 1979. "Considerations for an Evaluation Program of Instructional Quality." *CEDR Quarterly* 12: 8-12.

Braskamp, L.A. 1978. "Colleague Evaluation of Instruction." *Faculty Development and Evaluation in Higher Education* 4: 1-9.

Brinko, K.T. September/October 1993. "The Practice of Giving Feedback to Improve Teaching: What Is Effective?" *Journal of Higher Education* 64(5): 574-93.

Britt, N. Jr. 1982. "Faculty Attitudes About Colleague Evaluation of Teaching." *Dissertation Abstracts International* 42: 5034A. (University Microfilms No. 82-09886)

Brock, S.C. 1981. "Evaluation-Based Teacher Development." In *Handbook of Teacher Evaluation*, edited by J. Millman. Beverly Hills, Calif.: Sage.

Bryant, P.T. 1967. "By Their Fruits Ye Shall Know Them." *Journal of*

Higher Education 38: 326-30.

Bulcock, J.W. 1984. "Why Can't We Define Good Teaching?" Paper presented at the annual meeting of the Canadian Society for the Study of Education, Guelph, Ontario. ED 248 207. 41 pp. MF-01; PC-02.

Cancelli, A. 1987. "Methods for Arriving at Clinical Judgments in Peer Evaluation." Paper presented at the annual meeting of the American Educational Research Association, Washington, D.C. ED 282 924. 23 pp. MF-01; PC-01.

Carnegie Foundation for the Advancement of Teaching. 1986. Carnegie Survey. *Chronicle of Higher Education.*

———. 1990a. *Campus Life: In Search of Community.* Princeton, N.J.: Carnegie Foundation.

———. 1990b. *Scholarship Reconsidered: Priorities of the Professoriate.* Princeton, N.J.: Carnegie Foundation. ED 326 149. 151 pp. MF-01; PC not available EDRS.

Carroll, J.G., and S.R. Goldberg. 1989. "Teaching Consultants: A Collegial Approach to Better Teaching." *College Teaching* 37: 143-46.

Carroll, M.A., and J.C. Tyson. 1981. "Good Teachers Can Become Better." *Improving College and University Teaching* 29(2): 92-94.

Carton, A.S. 1988. "Linguistics 111." In *Turning Professors Into Teachers: A New Approach to Faculty Development and Student Learning,* by J. Katz and M. Henry. New York: American Council on Education/Macmillan.

Centra, J.A. May/June 1975. "Colleagues as Raters of Classroom Instruction." *Journal of Higher Education* 46: 327-37.

———. 1979. *Determining Faculty Effectiveness.* San Francisco: Jossey-Bass.

———. 1986. "Colleague Evaluation: The Critical Link." Paper presented at the annual meeting of the American Educational Research Association, San Francisco. ED 275 722. 6 pp. MF-01; PC-01.

———. 1993. *Reflective Faculty Evaluation: Enhancing Teaching and Determining Faculty Effectiveness.* San Francisco: Jossey-Bass.

Chenoweth, T. 1991. "Evaluating Exemplary Teaching." *Journal of Personnel Evaluation in Education* 4: 359-66.

Chickering, A.W. 1984. "Faculty Evaluation: Problems and Solutions." In *Changing Practices in Faculty Evaluation,* by P. Seldin. San Francisco: Jossey-Bass.

Cohen, P.A., and W.J. McKeachie. 1980. "The Role of Colleagues in the Evaluation of College Teaching." *Improving College and University Teaching* 28: 147-54.

Copeland, W.D., and R. Jamgochian. March/April 1985. "Colleague Training and Peer Review." *Journal of Teacher Education* 36: 18-21.

Cowen, D.L., G.L. Davis, and S.E. Bird. 1976. "Peer Review in Medical Education." *Journal of Medical Education* 51: 130-31.

Craig, J.R., D.L. Redfield, and G.R. Galluzzo. 1986. "Evaluating Effective Teaching in Colleges and Universities: How Far Have We Come?" Paper presented at the annual meeting of the American Evaluation Association, Kansas City, Mo. ED 282 888. 23 pp. MF-01; PC-01.

Cross, K.P. 1986a. "A Proposal to Improve Teaching—or—What 'Taking Teaching Seriously' Should Mean." *AAHE Bulletin* 39(1): 9-14.

———. 1986b. *Using Assessment to Improve Instruction.* Cambridge, Mass.: Harvard University. ED 284 896. 9 pp. MF-01; PC-01.

———. 1988. "In Search of Zippers." *AAHE Bulletin* 40(10): 3-7.

———. 1991. "College Teaching: What Do We Know About It?" *Innovative Higher Education* 16(1): 7-25.

Cross, K.P., and T.A. Angelo. 1988. *Classroom Assessment Techniques: A Handbook for Faculty.* Ann Arbor, Mich.: The University of Michigan National Center for Research for Improved Post-Secondary Teaching and Learning. ED 317 097. 166 pp. MF-01; PC-07.

Dennis, L.J. 1976. "Teacher Evaluation in Higher Education." *Liberal Education* 62: 437-43.

Dienst, E.R. 1981. *Evaluation by Colleagues.* San Francisco: University of California. ED 309 341. 6 pp. MF-01; PC-01.

Dornbusch, S.M. 1975. *Evaluation and the Exercise of Authority.* San Francisco: Jossey-Bass.

Doyle, K.O. Jr., and L.I. Crichton. 1978. "Student, Peer, and Self Evaluations of College Instruction." *Journal of Educational Psychology* 70: 815-26.

Dressel, P.L. 1976. "Faculty." In *Handbook of Academic Evaluation,* by P.L. Dressel, 331-75. San Francisco: Jossey-Bass.

Eble, K.E. 1972a. *Professors as Teachers.* San Francisco: Jossey-Bass.

———. 1972b. *The Recognition and Evaluation of Teaching.* Washington, D.C.: American Association of University Professors.

———. 1988. *The Craft of Teaching.* 2d ed. San Francisco: Jossey-Bass.

Eckert, R.E. 1950. "Ways of Evaluating College Teaching." *School and Society* 71: 65-69.

Edgerton, R. 1988. "All Roads Lead to Teaching." *AAHE Bulletin* 40(8): 3-9.

Edgerton, R., P. Hutchings, and K. Quinlan. 1991. *The Teaching Portfolio: Capturing the Scholarship of Teaching.* Washington, D.C.: American Association for Higher Education. ED 353 892. 62 pp. MF-01; PC not available EDRS.

Edwards, S. 1974. "A Modest Proposal for the Evaluation of Teaching." *Liberal Education* 60: 316-26.

Elbow, P. 1980. "One-to-One Faculty Development." In *Learning About Teaching,* edited by J.F. Noonan. New Directions for Teaching and Learning No. 4. San Francisco: Jossey-Bass.

———. 1986. *Embracing Contraries: Explorations in Learning and*

Teaching. New York: Oxford.

Erickson, G.G., and B.L. Erickson. September/October 1979. "Improving College Teaching." *Journal of Higher Education* 50: 670-83.

Fairweather, J.S. 1993. "Academic Values and Faculty Rewards." *Review of Higher Education* 17(1): 43-68.

Farmer, C.H. 1976. "Colleague Evaluation: The Silence Is Deafening." *Liberal Education* 62: 432-36.

Fitzgerald, M.J., and C.L. Grafton. 1981. "Comparisons and Implications of Peer and Student Evaluations for a Community College Faculty." *Community/Junior College Research Quarterly* 5: 331-37.

Freer, M., and J. Dawson. 1985. "DON'T Evaluate Your Teachers." *Phi Delta Kappan* 66: 720-22.

French-Lazovik, G. 1981. "Peer Review: Documentary Evidence in the Evaluation of Teaching." In *Handbook of Teacher Evaluation,* edited by J. Millman. Beverly Hills, Calif.: Sage.

Fuller, F.F., and B.A. Manning. 1973. "Self-Confrontation Reviewed: A Conceptualization for Video Playback in Teacher Education." *Review of Educational Research* 43: 469-528.

Gage, N.L. January/February 1961. "The Appraisal of College Teaching." *Journal of Higher Education* 32(1): 17-22.

Galm, J.A. 1985. "Welcome to Post-Tenure Review." *College Teaching* 33: 65-67.

Goldhammer, R. 1969. *Clinical Supervision.* New York: Holt, Rinehart and Winston.

Golin, S. 1990. "Four Arguments for Peer Evaluation and Student Interviews: The Master Faculty Program." *AAHE Bulletin* 43(4): 9-10.

Gray, P.J. 1991. "Using Assessment Data to Improve Teaching." In *Effective Practices for Improving Teaching,* edited by M. Theall and J. Franklin. New Directions for Teaching and Learning No. 48. San Francisco: Jossey-Bass.

Greenwood, G.E., and H.J. Ramagli Jr. November/December 1980. "Alternatives to Student Ratings of College Teaching." *Journal of Higher Education* 51: 673-84.

Gunn, B. 1982. "Evaluating Faculty Performance: A Holistic Approach." *Journal of the College and University Personnel Association* 34(4): 23-30.

Guthrie, E.R. 1949. "The Evaluation of Teaching." *The Educational Record* 30: 109-15.

Hart, F.R. 1987. "Teachers Observing Teachers." In *Teaching at an Urban University,* edited by J.H. Broderick. Boston: University of Massachusetts at Boston. ED 290 704. 77 pp. MF-01; PC-01.

Heller, D.A. 1989. *Peer Supervision: A Way of Professionalizing Teaching.* Bloomington, Ind.: Phi Delta Kappa.

Hind, R.R., S.M. Dornbusch, and W.R. Scott. 1974. "A Theory of Evaluation Applied to a University Faculty." *Sociology of Education* 47: 114-28.

Hodgkinson, H. 1972. "Unlock the Doors, Let Your Colleagues In: Faculty Reward and Assessment Systems." In *The Academic Department and Division Chairmen*, edited by J. Braun and T.A. Emmet. Detroit: Balamp.

———. 1974. "Adult Development: Implications for Faculty and Administrators." *Educational Record* 55: 263-74.

Hoyt, D.P., and G.S. Howard. 1978. "The Evaluation of Faculty Development Programs." *Research in Higher Education* 8: 25-38.

Hutchings, P. 1993. "Introducing Faculty Portfolios: Early Lessons From CUNY York College." *AAHE Bulletin* 45(9): 14-17.

Johnson, D.W., Johnson, R.T., and K.A. Smith. 1991. *Cooperative Learning: Increasing College Faculty Productivity*. ASHE–ERIC Higher Education Report No. 4. Washington, D.C.: Association for the Study of Higher Education. ED 343 465. 168 pp. MF-01; PC-07.

Jones, M.A. 1986. "Participatory Evaluation of a Departmental Peer Review Process for Awarding Merit Pay to University Faculty." *Dissertation Abstracts International* 48:0316A. (University Microfilms No. 87-11724)

Katz, J., and M. Henry. 1988. *Turning Professors Into Teachers: A New Approach to Faculty Development and Student Learning*. Phoenix: Oryx.

Keig, L.W. 1989. *Faculty Evaluation: Iowa Association of Independent Colleges and Universities*. Unpublished manuscript.

———. 1991. "A Study of Peer Involvement in the Formative Evaluation of Instruction in Higher Education." *Dissertation Abstracts International* 52: 5-1,593A (University Microfilms No. 91-31189).

Lacey, P.A. 1988. "Faculty Development and the Future of College Teaching." In *College Teaching and Learning: Preparing for New Commitments*, edited by R.E. Young and K.E. Eble. New Directions for Teaching and Learning No. 33. San Francisco: Jossey-Bass.

Ladd, E.C. Jr. 1979. "The Work Experience of American College Professors: Some Data and an Argument." *Current Issues in Higher Education* No. 2. Washington, D.C.: American Association for Higher Education.

Lawrence, J., and R. Blackburn. 1985. "Faculty Careers: Maturation, Demographic, and Historical Effects." *Research in Higher Education* 22: 135-54.

Lee, B.A. 1982. "Balancing Confidentiality and Disclosure in Faculty Peer Review: Impact on Title VII Litigation." *Journal of College and University Law* 9: 279-314.

Levinson-Rose, J., and R.J. Menges. 1981. "Improving College Teaching: A Critical Review of Research." *Review of Educational Research* 3: 403-34.

Licata, C.M. 1986. *Post-Tenure Faculty Evaluation: Opportunity or Threat?* ASHE-ERIC Higher Education Report No. 1. Washington, D.C.: Association for the Study of Higher Education. ED 270 009. 118 pp. MF-01; PC-05.

Lichty, R.W., and J.M. Peterson. 1979. *Peer Evaluations—A Necessary Part of Evaluating Teaching Effectiveness.* Duluth: University of Minnesota. ED 175 352. 7 pp. MF-01; PC-01.

Lindquist, J., ed. 1979. *Designing Teaching Improvement Programs.* Washington, D.C.: Council for the Advancement of Small Colleges.

Lowman, J. 1984. *Mastering the Techniques of Teaching.* San Francisco: Jossey-Bass.

Marques, T.E., D.M. Lane, and P.W. Dorfman. 1979. "Toward the Development of a System for Instructional Evaluation: Is There a Consensus Regarding What Constitutes Effective Teaching?" *Journal of Educational Psychology* 71: 840-49.

Maslow, A.H., and W. Zimmerman. 1956. "College Teaching Ability, Scholarly Activity and Personality." *The Journal of Educational Psychology* 47: 185-89.

Mathias, H., and D. Rutherford. 1982a. "Course Evaluation at Birmingham: Some Implications for the Evaluation of University Teaching." *Studies in Educational Evaluation* 7: 263-66.

———. 1982b. "Lecturers as Evaluators: The Birmingham Experience." *Studies in Higher Education* 7: 47-56.

Mathis, B.C. 1974. *Persuading the Institution to Experiment: Strategies for Seduction.* Occasional Paper No. 9, Center for the Teaching Professions. Evanston, Ill.: Northwestern University.

———. 1979a. "Academic Careers and Adult Development." In *Current Issues in Higher Education* No. 2, edited by R. Edgerton. Washington, D.C.: American Association for Higher Education.

———. 1979b. "The University Center." In *Designing Teaching Improvement Programs,* edited by J. Lindquist. Washington, D.C.: Council for the Advancement of Small Colleges.

Mauksch, H.O. 1980. "What Are the Obstacles to Improving Quality Teaching?" *Current Issues in Higher Education* No. 1: 49-56. Washington, D.C.: American Association for Higher Education.

McCarthey, S.J., and K.D. Peterson. 1988. "Peer Review of Materials in Public School Teacher Evaluation." *Journal of Personnel Evaluation in Education* 1: 259-67.

McDaniel, E.A. 1987. "Faculty Collaboration for Better Teaching: Adult Learning Principles Applied to Teaching Improvement." In *To Improve the Academy,* vol. 6, edited by J. Kurfiss. Stillwater, Okla.: New Forums Press.

McIntosh, T.H., and T.E. Van Koevering. 1986. "Six-Year Case Study of Faculty Peer Review, Merit Ratings, and Pay Awards in a Multidisciplinary Department." *Journal of the College and University Personnel Association* 37: 5-14.

McIntyre, C.J. 1978. *Peer Evaluation of Teaching.* Urbana-Champaign: University of Illinois. ED 180 295. 7 pp. MF-01; PC-01.

McIntyre, K.E. 1986. *Using Classroom Observation Data for Diagnosis Purposes.* Paper presented at the annual meeting of the American Educational Research Association, San Francisco. ED 275 731. 12 pp. MF-01; PC-01.

McKeachie, W.J. 1982. "The Rewards of Teaching." In *Motivating Professors to Teach Effectively,* edited by J.L. Bess. New Directions for Teaching and Learning, No. 10. San Francisco: Jossey-Bass.

————. 1986. *Teaching Tips: A Guidebook for Beginning College Teachers.* 8th ed. Lexington, Mass.: Heath.

————. 1987. "Can Evaluating Instruction Improve Teaching?" In *Techniques for Evaluating and Improving Instruction,* edited by L.M. Aleamoni. New Directions for Teaching and Learning, No. 31. San Francisco: Jossey- Bass.

Menges, R.J. 1980. "Teaching Improvement Strategies: How Effective Are They?" *Current Issues in Higher Education,* No. 1: 25-31. Washington, D.C.: American Association for Higher Education.

————. 1985. "Career-Span Faculty Development." *College Teaching* 33: 181-84.

————. 1987. "Colleagues As Catalysts for Change in Teaching." In *To Improve the Academy,* edited by J. Kurfiss: 83-93. Stillwater, Okla.: New Forums Press.

————. 1990. "Using Evaluation Information to Improve Instruction." In *How Administrators Can Improve Teaching,* by P. Seldin. San Francisco: Jossey-Bass.

————. 1991. "The Real World of Teaching Improvement: A Faculty Perspective." In *Effective Practices for Improving Teaching,* edited by M. Theall and J. Franklin. New Directions for Teaching and Learning, No. 48. San Francisco: Jossey-Bass.

Mengis, R.J., and B.C. Mathis. 1988. *Key Resources on Teaching, Learning, Curriculum, and Faculty Development.* San Francisco: Jossey-Bass.

Mikula, A.R. 1979. *Using Peers in Instructional Development.* Altoona: The Pennsylvania State University. ED 172 599. 14 pp. MF-01; PC-01.

Miller, L.H. Jr. September/October 1990. "Hubris in the Academy." *Change* 22(5): 9+.

Millman, J., ed. 1981. *Handbook of Teacher Evaluation.* Beverly Hills, Calif.: Sage.

Murray, H.G. 1975. "Predicting Student Ratings of College Teaching from Peer Ratings of Personality Types." *Teaching of Psychology* 2(2): 66-69.

New Jersey Institute for Collegiate Teaching and Learning. 1991. *Partners in Learning.* South Orange, N.J.: NJICTL, Seton Hall University.

Ottaway, R.N. 1991. "How Students Learn in a Management Class." In *The Teaching Portfolio: Capturing the Scholarship of Teaching*, edited by R. Edgerton, P. Hutchings, and K. Quinlan. Washington, D.C.: American Association for Higher Education.

Parsons, T. 1954. *The Social System*. New York: The Free Press.

Perlberg, A. 1983. "When Professors Confront Themselves: Toward a Theoretical Conceptualization of Video Self-Confrontation in Higher Education." *Higher Education* 12: 633-63.

Peterson, K., and D. Kauchek. 1982. *Teacher Evaluation: Perspectives, Practices, and Promises*. Salt Lake City: Center for Professional Practice, University of Utah. ED 233 996. 53 pp. MF-01; PC-03.

Peterson, M.W., and R. Blackburn. 1985. "Faculty Effectiveness: Meeting Institutional Needs and Expectations." *Review of Higher Education* 9: 21-34.

Pew Higher Education Research Program. May 1989. "The Business of the Business." *Policy Perspectives* 1: 1-7.

———. September 1990. "Back to Business." *Policy Perspectives* 3: 1-8.

———. September 1992. "Testimony From the Belly of the Whale." *Policy Perspectives* 4(3): 1-8.

Pittman, R.B., and J.R. Slate. 1989. "Faculty Evaluation: Some Conceptual Considerations." *Journal of Personnel Evaluation in Education* 3: 39-51.

Poch, R.K. 1993. *Academic Freedom in American Higher Education: Rights, Responsibilities, and Limitations*. ASHE-ERIC Higher Education Report No. 4. Washington, D.C.: The George Washington University, Graduate School of Education and Human Development. ED 366 263. 109 pp. MF-01; PC-05.

Prater, D.L. 1983. "What Counts as Effective University Teaching: The State of the Art." Paper presented at the annual meeting of the Southwest Educational Research Association, Houston. ED 227 149. 12 pp. MF-01; PC-01.

Razor, J.E. 1979. *The Evaluation of Administrators and Faculty Members—Or Evaluation of the "Boss" or Each Other*. Normal: Illinois State University. ED 180 355.

Rice, R.E., and S.I. Cheldolin. 1989. "The Knower and the Known: Making the Connection: Evaluation of the New Jersey Master Faculty Program." South Orange, N.J.: New Jersey Institute for Collegiate Teaching and Learning, Seton Hall University.

Riegle, R.P., and D.M. Rhodes. 1986. "Avoiding Mixed Metaphors in Faculty Evaluation." *College Teaching* 34: 123-28.

Romberg, E. 1985. "Description of Peer Evaluation within a Comprehensive Evaluation Program in a Dental School." *Instructional Evaluation* 8(1): 10-16.

Root, L.S. 1987. "Faculty Evaluation: Reliability of Peer Assessment of Research, Teaching, and Service." *Research in Higher Education*

26: 71-84.

Roper, S.S., T.E. Deal, and S. Dornbusch. 1976. "Collegial Evaluation of Classroom Teaching: Does it Work?" *Educational Research Quarterly* 1(1): 56-66.

Rorschach, E., and R. Whitney. 1986. "Relearning to Teach: Peer Observation as a Means of Professional Development for Teachers." *English Education* 18: 159-72.

Rutland, P. 1990. "Some Considerations Regarding Teaching Evaluations." *Political Science Teacher* 3(4): 1-2.

Sauter, R.C., and J.K. Walker. 1976. "A Theoretical Model for Faculty 'Peer' Evaluation." *American Journal of Pharmaceutical Education* 40: 165-66.

Schneider, L.S. 1975. *Faculty Opinion of the Spring 1974 Peer Evaluation.* Los Angeles: Los Angeles City College. ED 104 493. 24 pp. MF-01; PC-01.

Scriven, M.S. 1980. *The Evaluation of College Teaching.* Syracuse, N.Y.: National Council on States Inservice Education. Ed 203 729. 22 pp. MF-01; PC-01.

———. 1983. "Evaluation Ideologies." In *Evaluation Models: Viewpoints on Educational and Human Services Evaluation,* edited by G.R. Madaus, M.S. Scriven, and D.L. Stufflebeam. Boston: Kluver-Nijhof.

———. 1985. "New Frontiers of Evaluation." *Evaluation Practices* 7: 7-44.

———. 1987. "Validity in Personnel Evaluation." *Journal of Personnel Evaluation in Education* 1: 9-23.

Seldin, P. 1980. *Successful Faculty Evaluation Programs.* Crugers, N.Y.: Coventry Press.

———. 1984. *Changing Practices in Faculty Evaluation.* San Francisco: Jossey-Bass.

———. 1990. *How Administrators Can Improve Teaching.* San Francisco: Jossey-Bass.

———. 1991. *The Teaching Portfolio: A Practical Guide to Improved Performance and Promotion/Tenure Decisions.* Bolton, Mass.: Anker.

———. 1993a. "How Colleges Evaluate Professors." *AAHE Bulletin* 46(2): 6+.

———. 1993b. *Successful Use of Teaching Portfolios.* Bolton, Mass.: Anker.

———. July 21, 1993c. "The Use and Abuse of Student Ratings of Professors." *Chronicle of Higher Education:* A40.

Shatzky, J., and R. Silberman. 1986. "Master-Students: A Teaching Technique." *Journal of College Science Teaching* 16: 119-20.

Sherman, T.M., L.P. Armistead, F. Fowler, M.A. Barksdale, and G. Reif. January/February 1987. "The Quest for Excellence in University Teaching." *Journal of Higher Education* 48: 66-84.

Shulman, L.S. 1987. "Knowledge and Teaching: Foundations of the New Reforms." *Harvard Educational Review* 57(1): 1-22.

———. 1988. "A Union of Insufficiencies: Strategies for Teacher Assessment in a Period of Education Reform." *Educational Leadership* 46(3): 36-41.

———. 1989. "Toward a Pedagogy of Substance." *AAHE Bulletin* 41(10): 8-13.

———. November/December 1993. "Teaching as Community Property: Putting an End to Pedagogical Solitude." *Change* 25(6): 6-7.

Singh, R. 1984. "Peer-Evaluation: A Process That Could Enhance the Self-Esteem and Professional Growth of Teachers." *Education* 105(1): 73-75.

Skoog, G. March/April 1980. "Improving College Teaching Through Peer Observation." *Journal of Teacher Education* 31: 23-25.

Smith, A. 1985. "The Challenge of Peer Evaluation." *Instructional Evaluation* 8(1): 2-3.

Smith, G. 1987. "The Practitioners of Staff Development." *Journal for Higher Education* 1(1): 58-67.

Smith, H.L., and B.E. Walvoord. 1993. "Certifying Teaching Excellence: An Alternative Paradigm to the Teaching Award." *AAHE Bulletin* 46(2): 3+.

Smith, M.J., and M. LaCelle-Peterson. 1991. "The Professor as Active Learner: Lessons from the New Jersey Master Faculty Plan." *To Improve the Academy* 10: 271-78.

Smith, M.R. 1981. "Protecting the Confidentiality of Faculty Peer Review Records: Department of Labor v. The University of California." *Journal of College and University Law* 8: 20-53.

Smith, P., C. Hausken, H. Kovacevich, and M. McGuire. 1988. *Alternatives for Developing Teacher Effectiveness.* Seattle: School of Education, Seattle Pacific University. ED 301 115. 22 pp. MF-01; PC-01.

Soderberg, L.O. 1985. "Dominance of Research and Publications: An Unrelenting Tyranny." *College Teaching* 33: 168-72.

———. March 1986. "A Credible Model: Evaluating Classroom Teaching in Higher Education." *Instructional Evaluation* 8: 13-27.

Sorcinelli, M.D. 1984. "An Approach to Colleague Evaluation of Classroom Instruction." *Journal of Instructional Development* 7: 11-17.

Spaights, E., and E. Bridges. 1986. "Peer Evaluations for Salary Increases and Promotions Among College and University Faculty Members." *North Central Association Quarterly* 60: 403-10.

Stevens, E. 1988. "Tinkering With Teaching." *Review of Higher Education* 12: 63-78.

Stevens, J.J. 1985. "Legal Issues in the Use of Peer Evaluation." *Instructional Evaluation* 8(1): 17-21.

Stevens, J.J., and L.M. Aleamoni. 1985. "Issues in the Development of Peer Evaluation Systems." *Instructional Evaluation* 8(1): 4-9.

Stodolsky, S.S. November 1984. "Teacher Evaluation: The Limits of Looking." *Educational Researcher* 13: 11-18.

Stoner, M., and L. Martin. 1993. *Talking About Teaching Across the Disciplines: How Cognitive Peer Coaching Makes It Happen.* Paper presented at the 79th annual meeting of the Speech Communication Association, Miami.

Study Group on the Conditions of Excellence in American Higher Education. 1984. *Involvement in Learning: Realizing the Potential of American Higher Education.* Washington D.C.: National Institute of Education/U.S. Department of Education. ED 246 833. 127 pp. MF-01; PC-06.

Stumpf, W.E. 1980. "Peer Review." *Science* 207: 822-23.

Swanson, F.A., and D.J. Sisson. 1971. "The Development, Evaluation, and Utilization of Departmental Faculty Appraisal System." *Journal of Industrial Teacher Education* 9(1): 64-79.

Sweeney, J.M.W. 1976. "A Report on the Development and Use of a Faculty Peer Evaluation/Development Program." *Dissertation Abstracts International* 37: 5458A. (University Microfilms No. 76-30408)

Sweeney, J.M., and A.F. Grasha. 1979. "Improving Teaching Through Faculty Development Triads." *Educational Technology* 19: 54-57.

Tobias, S. March/April 1986. "Peer Perspectives on the Teaching of Science." *Change* 18(2): 36-41.

Uguroglu, M.E., and M.M. Dwyer. 1981. "Staff Review System." *Improving College and University Teaching* 29: 121-24.

Ward, M.D., D.C. Clark, and G.V. Harrison. 1981. *The Observation Effect in Classroom Visitation.* Macomb: Western Illinois University. Ed 204 384. 21 pp. MF-01; PC-01.

Webb, W.B. 1955. "The Problem of Obtaining Negative Nominations in Peer Ratings." *Personnel Psychology* 8: 61-63.

Weimer, M. 1987. "Translating Evaluation Results into Teaching Improvements." *AAHE Bulletin* 39(8): 8-11.

———. 1990. *Improving College Teaching: Strategies for Developing Instructional Effectiveness.* San Francisco: Jossey-Bass.

Weimer, M., M.M. Kerns, and J.L. Parrett. 1988. "Instructional Observation: Caveats, Concerns, and Ways to Compensate." *Studies in Higher Education* 13: 285-93.

Weimer, M., J.L. Parrett, and M. Kerns. 1988. *How Am I Teaching?* Madison, Wis.: Magna.

Weinbach, R.W., and J.L. Randolph. 1984. "Peer Review for Tenure and Promotion in Professional Schools." *Improving College and University Teaching* 32: 81-86.

Wherry, R.J., and D.H. Fryer. 1945. "Buddy Ratings: Popularity Contest or Leadership Criteria?" *Personnel Psychology* 2: 147-59.

Wilkinson, J. 1991. "Helping Students Write About History." In *The*

Teaching Portfolio, edited by R. Edgerton, P. Hutchings, and K. Quinlan, 37-39. Washington, D.C.: American Association for Higher Education.

Wilson, R.C. March/April 1986. "Faculty Teaching: Effective Use of Student Evaluations." *Journal of Higher Education* 57: 197-211.

Wilson, R.C., E.R. Dienst, and N.L. Watson. 1973. "Characteristics of Effective College Teachers as Perceived by Their Colleagues." *Journal of Educational Measurement* 10: 31-37.

Wolansky, W.D. 1976. "A Multiple Approach to Faculty Evaluation." *Education* 97: 81-96.

Wood, P.H. 1977. *The Description and Evaluation of a College Department's Faculty Rating System.* Bowling Green, Ohio: Bowling Green State University. ED 142 128. 26 pp. MF-01; PC-02.

————. 1978. *Student and Peer Ratings of College Teaching and Peer Ratings of Research and Service: Four Years of Departmental Evaluation.* Bowling Green, Ohio: Bowling Green State University. ED 155 218. 59 pp. MF-01; PC-03.

Woolwine, D.E. 1988. *New Jersey Master Faculty Program Research Report.* South Orange, N.J.: NJICTL, Seton Hall University.

Yarbrough, D.B. 1988. "A Cognitive Psychological Perspective on Teacher Evaluation." *Journal of Personnel Evaluation in Education* 2: 215-28.

INDEX

A

academic conventions that undermine teaching improvement efforts, 15

academic freedom, barrier to teacher evaluation, xiii, 97-98

academic values

        as disincentives to formative peer review, 103-104

        as incentives to formative peer review, 105-106

Abrami (1985), 15, 36, 37, 113

attitudes and perceptions as incentives, 105-108

Arubayi (1987), 117

American Association for Higher Education, 91

Austin (1992a&b), 87, 122-123, 129, 131

audiotape, use of, 66

academic administrators. *See also* summative and formative evaluations

        not likely to be sought to help in teaching evaluation, 3

B

Baldwin (1990), 18

Batista (1976), 19, 29, 31, 33

Bergman (1979, 1980), 54, 102, 116

Bergquist and Phillips (1975), 44-45

Bergquist and Phillips model of classroom observation, 44

Blackburn (1991), 143

blind review of tests, recommendations on, 32

born and not made, mistaken notion for teaching effectiveness, 3

Brandenburg, Braskamp, and Ory (1979), 58

Braskamp (1978), 102

Brinko (1993), 58, 115, 137

Britt (1982), 56, 118, 128

Brock (1981), 111, 116

Bryant (1967), 65

Bulcock (1984), 100, 126

C

California State University, Sacramento, 83-84, 92-94

Cancelli (1987), 16, 112

Centra (1975), 54 , 102

Centra (1978), 102

Centra (1986), 59, 68, 103, 114, 116

Chickering (1984), 126

classroom observation. *See also* direct classroom observation

        guide to. *See* Sorcinelli guidelines

        how long should be continued, 53

        how many constitute valid sample, 52

        number of visits, 93

        potential for formative evaluation, 21

faculty evaluation. *See also* formative and summative evaluation
    best time for, 29
    competencies, methods that don't assess range of, 98-101
    criteria, 35-36
    criticism of, xiii
    data sources should be diverse and used in combination
        for, 139-142
    evaluators, must keep summative and formative
        separate, 138-139
    faculty, must come from, 137
    formal systematic best, 8
    goal of this report, 1-2
    improvement of, xiv
    non related fields, should be from, 50-52
    questions to answer before beginning, 20
    representativeness of, 108
    roles, classification of, 30
    summative and formative should be kept separate, 134
    within discipline, should be from, 50-52
faculty morale and collegiality, improvement in, 128-132
Fairleigh Dickinson University, 86
Freer and Dawson (1985), 111
"formative atmosphere," 138
Formative evaluation
    academic administrators should have supportive
        role in, 21
    benefits of, 12
    definition of, 12
    developing and sustaining, recommendations for, 111
    function or purpose of, 14, 134
    model for sources of, 136
    need for, 13
    nonjudgmental descriptions needed, 135
    personnel decisions, should not be used in making, 13
    positive effect on faculty morale, 128
    programs need greater documentation, 143
    research needed on peer evaluation, 143
    threats to reliability and validity, 53-54
    year-long programs every four or five years
        suggested, 135, 137

G
Gage (1961), 101
Galm (1985), 85, 130
goals of this report, listing of, 1-2
Golin (1990), 90, 124
Gordon College, 70-71

Gray (1991), 113
Greenwood and Ramagli (1980), 20

H

"halo effects," 32, 37
Hart (1987), 29, 42-44, 100
Harvard College, 87
Heller (1989), 110, 128

I

Instructional methods and materials, assess effectiveness of, 31
instructional improvement
      evaluation for, 52
      planning of requires involvement of faculty, 110-111
      requires faculty and administrative support, 131
instructor evaluations of student academic work
      assessment of, 31-32, 64-68, 141
      guide to assessment, 67
      problematical, 68
integrative process of instructional evaluation, 32-34
interpreters and integrators of information, faculty as, 117-119

J

Jones (1986), 102

K

Katz and Henry (1988), 6, 29, 53, 66, 73, 88, 94, 109
Keig (1991), 56, 118
knowledge and learning construct, 114
knowledge of subject not sufficient to teach it, 3

L

Lee (1982), 8
lernfreiheit, 138
Licata (1986), 11
Ladd (1979), 107
Lichty and Peterson (1979), 55
Levinson-Rose and Menges (1981), 122
Lilly Endowment Teaching Fellows Program, 87-88
      tenure success, value in, 131
      formative peer evaluation improved morale, 129-130
      study of effectiveness of, 122-123

M

Mathias and Rutherford (1982a&b), 50, 82
Mathis (1974), 38-39
McCarthey and Peterson (1988), 60, 63
McDaniel (1987), 18, 57, 85

McDaniel's three-stage model of formative evaluation of
    teaching, 57-58, 85
McIntyre (1986), 115
McKeachie (1986), 15, 21, 33, 100
Menges (1980, 1985, 1991), 7, 12, 68
Menges (1990), 128
Menges (1987), 17, 59
Menges and Mathis (1988), 113
Miller (1990), 7
motivational theory and evaluation, need research on linkage
    between, 143
Multi-Institution programs, 87-91

N

New Jersey Master Faculty Program. *See* Partners in Learning
New York University, 81-82, 92, 93

O

observables. *See* effective teaching, skills associated with
observations of teaching. *See* classroom observation
Omnibus Personality Inventory, 74
OPI. *See* Omnibus Personality Inventory.
Ottaway (1991), 87

P

Parsons (1954), Talcott, 102
Partners in Learning, 88-91, 92-94, 123-125
        why and how it works, 90-91
"pedagogy of substance," 5
"pedagogical content knowledge," 138
peer observation, common to different programs, 95
peer review in teaching
        aspects best assessed by faculty, 34
        collaboration as indicator of faculty vitality, 18
        example of evaluation of, 17
        methods used, 41
        multi-institution study of, 91
        rare, 16
        rationale for, 14, 15
        roles in, classification of, 30
        should not be the only component of teaching review, 140
        silent observer role, 94
        student observations and ratings, as only, 33-34
        team approach, 92
        threats to reliability and validity, 53
Perlberg (1983), 55, 57, 115
PIL. *See* Partners in Learning
Pittman and Slate (1989), 20, 106

Post-Observation Conference Guide. *See* Sorcinelli guidelines
Pre-Observation Conference Guide. *See* Sorcinelli guidelines
Professors' Peer Coaching Program, 83, 84
        compares reality with perception, 84

R

reciprocity, strength in peer review of teaching, 92
research needed on formative peer evaluation, 143
reward system as cause for teaching neglect, 2-3
rhetorical dimension of teaching, 43
Rice and Cheldelin (1989), 124
risk takers, successful teachers are, 24
Romberg (1985), 24
        model, 24-25
Roper, Deal, and Dornbusch (1976), 25
        model, 25-27
Rorschach and Whitney (1986), 81

S

San Jose State University, 85-86, 92, 94
Schulman, 3-6
Scriven (1980), 8, 50, 62, 66
Scriven (1985, 1987), 29, 30, 32, 35-36, 100
secondary indicators. *See* effective teaching, skills associated with
Seldin (1984), 29, 34, 59, 108, 125
Seldin (1991), 69
self-evaluation, essential for improvement in teaching, 18
Shatzky and Silberman (1986), 80
Shulman (1987), 109, 114, 138, 139
Shulman (1993), 50
Shulman, new in progress multi institutional study of, 91
Skoog (1980), 110, 130
Smith (1981), 8
Smith (1988), 56, 63, 66
Smith and Walvoord (1993), 15, 112
Soderberg (1986), 8, 29, 31, 32
Soderberg model, 22
        constituencies that can tell about faculty strengths and
           weakness, 24
        identifies most appropriate constituency evaluation
           area, 29
        interdependent processes, 22
        temporal phases, 23-24
Sorcinelli (1984), 45, 50, 116
Sorcinelli guidelines
        listing of, 45-49
        problems in using, 4
Stanford University, 91

physical-temporal setting of, 42-43
reasons for being less-than-effective, 2-7
rewards and incentives of institution should value, 142-143
self-evaluation, essential for improvement of, 18
skills associated with effective, 100
tenure success, improvement in, 131-132
tests, evaluation of preparation and grading procedures, 66
Texas Tech University, 76-77, 92, 93
training in supervision-evaluation, 115-117
awareness increase, 116
background necessary for trainer, 116
evaluation transmission, procedure on, 115
interrater reliability, improvement of, 115
necessary for formative evaluation by peers, 137-138
skills to be acquired, 116-117

U

university centers, unlikely source of effective teaching
improvement, 6
University of Birmingham, 82-83, 92, 93
University of Cincinnati, 75-76, 92, 93
University of Hartford, 85
University of Kentucky College of Medicine, 77-78, 86, 92
University of Maryland, 24
University of New York, Cortland, 80, 92-94
University of New York, Stony Brook, 73-75, 88, 92-94
University of Northern Iowa College of Education, xiv
University of South Carolina, 78, 93

V

Videotaping of Classes, 55-59
example of, 85
justification for, 55
motivating faculty to approve, 57
not used just as an alternative to direct classroom
observation, 140
provide clues to student responses, 56
self-confrontational nature of, 58

W

Ward, Clark, and Harrison (1981), 101
Weimer (1987), 14
Weimer (1990), 42, 51
Weimer, Kerns, and Parrett (1988), 13-14, 50, 52)
Wood (1977, 1978), 53, 54

Y

Yarbrough (1988), 4-5

ASHE-ERIC HIGHER EDUCATION REPORTS

Since 1983, the Association for the Study of Higher Education (ASHE) and the Educational Resources Information Center (ERIC) Clearinghouse on Higher Education, a sponsored project of the School of Education and Human Development at The George Washington University, have cosponsored the *ASHE-ERIC Higher Education Report* series. The 1994 series is the twenty-third overall and the sixth to be published by the School of Education and Human Development at the George Washington University.

Each monograph is the definitive analysis of a tough higher education problem, based on thorough research of pertinent literature and institutional experiences. Topics are identified by a national survey. Noted practitioners and scholars are then commissioned to write the reports, with experts providing critical reviews of each manuscript before publication.

Eight monographs (10 before 1985) in the ASHE-ERIC Higher Education Report series are published each year and are available on individual and subscription bases. To order, use the order form on the last page of this book.

Qualified persons interested in writing a monograph for the ASHE-ERIC Higher Education Reports are invited to submit a proposal to the National Advisory Board. As the preeminent literature review and issue analysis series in higher education, we can guarantee wide dissemination and national exposure for accepted candidates. Execution of a monograph requires at least a minimal familiarity with the ERIC database, including *Resources in Education* and *Current Index to Journals in Education*. The objective of these Reports is to bridge conventional wisdom with practical research. Prospective authors are strongly encouraged to call Dr. Fife at 800-773-3742.

For further information, write to
   ASHE-ERIC Higher Education Reports
   The George Washington University
   1 Dupont Circle, Suite 630
   Washington, DC 20036
Or phone (202) 296-2597, toll-free: 800-773-ERIC.
   Write or call for a complete catalog.

ADVISORY BOARD

Scott Rickard
Association of College Unions–International

G. Jeremiah Ryan
Harford Community College

Patricia A. Spencer
Riverside Community College

Frances Stage
Indiana University–Bloomington

Ellen Switkes
University of California–Oakland

Carolyn J. Thompson
State University of New York–Buffalo

Caroline Turner
University of Minnesota–Twin Cities

Sheila L. Weiner
Board of Overseers of Harvard College

Richard A. Yanikoski
De Paul University

REVIEW PANEL

Charles Adams
University of Massachusetts–Amherst

Louis Albert
American Association for Higher Education

Richard Alfred
University of Michigan

Philip G. Altbach
State University of New York–Buffalo

Marilyn J. Amey
University of Kansas

Louis C. Attinasi, Jr.
University of Houston

Robert J. Barak
Iowa State Board of Regents

Alan Bayer
Virginia Polytechnic Institute and State University

John P. Bean
Indiana University

John M. Braxton
Vanderbilt University

Peter McE. Buchanan
Council for Advancement and
    Support of Education

John A. Centra
Syracuse University

Arthur W. Chickering
George Mason University

Shirley M. Clark
Oregon State System of Higher Education

Darrel A. Clowes
Virginia Polytechnic Institute and State University

John W. Creswell
University of Nebraska–Lincoln

Deborah DiCroce
Piedmont Virginia Community College

Richard Duran
University of California

Kenneth C. Green
University of Southern California

Edward R. Hines
Illinois State University

Marsha W. Krotseng
West Virginia State College and University Systems

George D. Kuh
Indiana University–Bloomington

Daniel T. Layzell
University of Wisconsin System

Meredith Ludwig
American Association of State Colleges and Universities

Mantha V. Mehallis
Florida Atlantic University

Robert J. Menges
Northwestern University

Toby Milton
Essex Community College

James R. Mingle
State Higher Education Executive Officers

Gary Rhoades
University of Arizona

G. Jeremiah Ryan
Harford Community College

Mary Ann Sagaria
Ohio State University

Daryl G. Smith
Claremont Graduate School

William Tierney
Pennsylvania State University

Susan Twombly
University of Kansas

Harold Wechsler
University of Rochester

Michael J. Worth
George Washington University

RECENT TITLES

1994 ASHE-ERIC Higher Education Reports

1. The Advisory Committee Advantage: Creating an Effective
   Strategy for Programmatic Improvement
   by Lee Teitel

1993 ASHE-ERIC Higher Education Reports

1. The Department Chair: New Roles, Responsibilities and
   Challenges
   Alan T. Seagren, John W. Creswell, and Daniel W. Wheeler

2. Sexual Harassment in Higher Education: From Conflict to
   Community
   Robert O. Riggs, Patricia H. Murrell, and JoAnn C. Cutting

3. Chicanos in Higher Education: Issues and Dilemmas for the
   21st Century
   by Adalberto Aguirre, Jr., and Ruben O. Martinez

4. Academic Freedom in American Higher Education: Rights,
   Responsibilities, and Limitations
   by Robert K. Poch

5. Making Sense of the Dollars: The Costs and Uses of Faculty
   Compensation
   by Kathryn M. Moore and Marilyn J. Amey

6. Enhancing Promotion, Tenure and Beyond: Faculty Socialization
   as a Cultural Process
   by William G. Tierney and Robert A. Rhoads

7. New Perspectives for Student Affairs Professionals: Evolving
   Realities, Responsibilities and Roles
   by Peter H. Garland and Thomas W. Grace

8. Turning Teaching Into Learning: The Role of Student Responsibility in the Collegiate Experience
   by Todd M. Davis and Patricia Hillman Murrell

1992 ASHE-ERIC Higher Education Reports

1. The Leadership Compass: Values and Ethics in Higher Education
   John R. Wilcox and Susan L. Ebbs

2. Preparing for a Global Community: Achieving an International
   Perspective in Higher Education
   Sarah M. Pickert

3. Quality: Transforming Postsecondary Education
   Ellen Earle Chaffee and Lawrence A. Sherr

4. Faculty Job Satisfaction: Women and Minorities in Peril
   Martha Wingard Tack and Carol Logan Patitu

5. Reconciling Rights and Responsibilities of Colleges and Students: Offensive Speech, Assembly, Drug Testing, and Safety
   Annette Gibbs

6. Creating Distinctiveness: Lessons from Uncommon Colleges and Universities
   Barbara K. Townsend, L. Jackson Newell, and Michael D. Wiese

7. Instituting Enduring Innovations: Achieving Continuity of Change in Higher Education
   Barbara K. Curry

8. Crossing Pedagogical Oceans: International Teaching Assistants in U.S. Undergraduate Education
   Rosslyn M. Smith, Patricia Byrd, Gayle L. Nelson, Ralph Pat Barrett, and Janet C. Constantinides

1991 ASHE-ERIC Higher Education Reports

1. Active Learning: Creating Excitement in the Classroom
   Charles C. Bonwell and James A. Eison

2. Realizing Gender Equality in Higher Education: The Need to Integrate Work/Family Issues
   Nancy Hensel

3. Academic Advising for Student Success: A System of Shared Responsibility
   Susan H. Frost

4. Cooperative Learning: Increasing College Faculty Instructional Productivity
   David W. Johnson, Roger T. Johnson, and Karl A. Smith

5. High School–College Partnerships: Conceptual Models, Programs, and Issues
   Arthur Richard Greenberg

6. Meeting the Mandate: Renewing the College and Departmental Curriculum
   William Toombs and William Tierney

7. Faculty Collaboration: Enhancing the Quality of Scholarship and Teaching
   Ann E. Austin and Roger G. Baldwin

8. Strategies and Consequences: Managing the Costs in Higher Education
   John S. Waggaman

1990 ASHE-ERIC Higher Education Reports

1. The Campus Green: Fund Raising in Higher Education
   Barbara E. Brittingham and Thomas R. Pezzullo

2. The Emeritus Professor: Old Rank - New Meaning
   James E. Mauch, Jack W. Birch, and Jack Matthews

3. "High Risk" Students in Higher Education: Future Trends
   Dionne J. Jones and Betty Collier Watson

4. Budgeting for Higher Education at the State Level: Enigma, Paradox, and Ritual
   Daniel T. Layzell and Jan W. Lyddon

5. Proprietary Schools: Programs, Policies, and Prospects
   John B. Lee and Jamie P. Merisotis

6. College Choice: Understanding Student Enrollment Behavior
   Michael B. Paulsen

7. Pursuing Diversity: Recruiting College Minority Students
   Barbara Astone and Elsa Nuñez-Wormack

8. Social Consciousness and Career Awareness: Emerging Link in Higher Education
   John S. Swift, Jr.

1989 ASHE-ERIC Higher Education Reports

1. Making Sense of Administrative Leadership: The 'L' Word in Higher Education
   Estela M. Bensimon, Anna Neumann, and Robert Birnbaum

2. Affirmative Rhetoric, Negative Action: African-American and Hispanic Faculty at Predominantly White Universities
   Valora Washington and William Harvey

3. Postsecondary Developmental Programs: A Traditional Agenda with New Imperatives
   Louise M. Tomlinson

4. The Old College Try: Balancing Athletics and Academics in Higher Education
   John R. Thelin and Lawrence L. Wiseman

5. The Challenge of Diversity: Involvement or Alienation in the Academy?
   Daryl G. Smith

6. Student Goals for College and Courses: A Missing Link in Assessing and Improving Academic Achievement
   Joan S. Stark, Kathleen M. Shaw, and Malcolm A. Lowther

7. The Student as Commuter: Developing a Comprehensive Institutional Response
   Barbara Jacoby

8. Renewing Civic Capacity: Preparing College Students for Service and Citizenship
   Suzanne W. Morse

1988 ASHE-ERIC Higher Education Reports

1. The Invisible Tapestry: Culture in American Colleges and Universities
   George D. Kuh and Elizabeth J. Whitt

2. Critical Thinking: Theory, Research, Practice, and Possibilities
   Joanne Gainen Kurfiss

3. Developing Academic Programs: The Climate for Innovation
   Daniel T. Seymour

4. Peer Teaching: To Teach is To Learn Twice
   Neal A. Whitman

5. Higher Education and State Governments: Renewed Partnership, Cooperation, or Competition?
   Edward R. Hines

6. Entrepreneurship and Higher Education: Lessons for Colleges, Universities, and Industry
   James S. Fairweather

7. Planning for Microcomputers in Higher Education: Strategies for the Next Generation
   Reynolds Ferrante, John Hayman, Mary Susan Carlson, and Harry Phillips

8. The Challenge for Research in Higher Education: Harmonizing Excellence and Utility
   Alan W. Lindsay and Ruth T. Neumann

1987 ASHE-ERIC Higher Education Reports

1. Incentive Early Retirement Programs for Faculty: Innovative Responses to a Changing Environment
   Jay L. Chronister and Thomas R. Kepple, Jr.

2. Working Effectively with Trustees: Building Cooperative Campus Leadership
   Barbara E. Taylor

3. Formal Recognition of Employer-Sponsored Instruction: Conflict and Collegiality in Postsecondary Education
   Nancy S. Nash and Elizabeth M. Hawthorne

4. Learning Styles: Implications for Improving Educational Practices
   Charles S. Claxton and Patricia H. Murrell

5. Higher Education Leadership: Enhancing Skills through Professional Development Programs
   Sharon A. McDade

6. Higher Education and the Public Trust: Improving Stature in Colleges and Universities
   Richard L. Alfred and Julie Weissman

7. College Student Outcomes Assessment: A Talent Development Perspective
   Maryann Jacobi, Alexander Astin, and Frank Ayala, Jr.

8. Opportunity from Strength: Strategic Planning Clarified with Case Examples
   Robert G. Cope

1986 ASHE-ERIC Higher Education Reports

1. Post-tenure Faculty Evaluation: Threat or Opportunity?
   Christine M. Licata

2. Blue Ribbon Commissions and Higher Education: Changing Academe from the Outside
   Janet R. Johnson and Laurence R. Marcus

3. Responsive Professional Education: Balancing Outcomes and Opportunities
   Joan S. Stark, Malcolm A. Lowther, and Bonnie M.K. Hagerty

4. Increasing Students' Learning: A Faculty Guide to Reducing Stress among Students
   Neal A. Whitman, David C. Spendlove, and Claire H. Clark

5. Student Financial Aid and Women: Equity Dilemma?
   Mary Moran

6. The Master's Degree: Tradition, Diversity, Innovation
   Judith S. Glazer

7. The College, the Constitution, and the Consumer Student: Implications for Policy and Practice
   Robert M. Hendrickson and Annette Gibbs

8. Selecting College and University Personnel: The Quest and the Question
   Richard A. Kaplowitz

*Out-of-print. Available through EDRS. Call 1-800-443-ERIC.

ORDER FORM 94-2

Quantity   **Amount**

_____ Please begin my subscription to the 1994 *ASHE-ERIC Higher Education Reports* at $98.00, 31% off the cover price, starting with Report 1, 1994. Includes shipping. _____

_____ Please send a complete set of the 1993 *ASHE-ERIC Higher Education Reports* at $98.00, 31% off the cover price. Please add shipping charge, below. _____

Individual reports are avilable at the following prices:
1993 and 1994, $18.00; 1988-1992, $17.00; 1980-1987, $15.00

SHIPPING CHARGES
For orders of more than 50 books, please call for shipping information.

	Total Quantity:	*1, 2 or 3 books*	*Ea. addl. book*
U.S., 48 Contiguous States			
Ground:		$3.75	$0.15
2nd Day*:		8.25	1.10
Next Day*:		18.00	1.60
Alaska & Hawaii (2nd Day Only)*:		13.25	1.40

U.S. Territories and Foreign Countries: Please call for shipping information.
*Order will be shipping within 24 hours of request.
All prices shown on this form are subject to change.

PLEASE SEND ME THE FOLLOWING REPORTS:

Quantity	Report No.	Year	Title	Amount

Please check one of the following:
☐ Check enclosed, payable to GWU–ERIC.
☐ Purchase order attached ($45.00 minimum).
☐ Charge my credit card indicated below:
   ☐ Visa   ☐ MasterCard

Subtotal: _____
Shipping: _____
Total Due: _____

Expiration Date _____

Name _____

Title _____

Institution _____

Address _____

City _____ State _____ Zip _____

Phone _____ Fax _____ Telex _____

Signature _____ Date _____

SEND ALL ORDERS TO: ASHE-ERIC Higher Education Reports
The George Washington University
One Dupont Cir., Ste. 630, Washington, DC 20036-1183
Phone: (202) 296-2597 • Toll-free: 800-773-ERIC